SEASONS AT
EAGLE POND

SEASONS

AT

EAGLE

POND

Donald
Hall

Illustrations by
Thomas W. Nason

TICKNOR & FIELDS
NEW YORK
1987

Library of Congress Cataloging-in-Publication Data

Hall, Donald, date.
Seasons at Eagle Pond.

1. Hall, Donald, 1928–   . 2. Poets, American—20th century—Biography. 3. Farm life—New Hampshire. 4. New Hampshire—Social life and customs. I. Title.
PS3515.S3152Z47   1987   811'.54 [B]   87–10101
ISBN 0–89919–542–3

Printed in the United States of America

First Edition

P 10 9 8 7 6 5 4 3 2 1

The author is grateful for permission to reprint the essays in this book. "Winter" originally appeared in the exhibition catalogue *Winter*, published by the Hood Museum of Art, Dartmouth College, in the winter of 1986 and available through the University Press of New England, Hanover, New Hampshire. The essay also appeared, in a somewhat altered form, in *Harper's Magazine*. "Spring" is reprinted from *The Boston Globe Magazine*. "Old Roses and Birdsong" ("Summer") was first published in *Harper's Magazine*. Copyright © 1987 by *Harper's Magazine*. All rights reserved. Reprinted in the August issue by special permission. "Fall Ascendant: Reveries of an Autumn Amorist" is from *Harper's Magazine*. Copyright © 1986 by *Harper's Magazine*. All rights reserved. Reprinted from the October issue by special permission.

The author and publisher wish to thank Margaret W. Nason for permission to reproduce the illustrations. Some of the woodcuts previously appeared in *You Come Too* by Robert Frost, published by Holt, Rinehart and Winston in 1959.

for Edna and Ansel

Winter

In New Hampshire we know ourselves by Winter—in snow, in cold, in darkness. For some of us the first true snow begins it; for others Winter begins with the first bruising assault of zero weather. There is yet another sort, light-lovers, for whom Winter begins with dark's onset in mid-August. If we wake as we ought to at 5:30, we begin waking in darkness, and dawn turns throaty with the ululations of photophiliacs, noctophobics, some of whom are fanatical enough to begin lamentation late in the month of June—when dawn arrives at 4:32 A.M. and the day before it arrived at 4:31:30. On June 22 my wife Jane exchanges postcards of commiseration with a fellow in Michigan who is another amorist of light. Fortunately this mountain has an upside as well as a downside. When in January daylight lasts half a minute longer every day, Jane's faint green leaves take on color; she leans south toward Kearsarge and the low, brief but lengthening pale Winter sun. An observer can spy the faint buds that will burst into snowdrops and daffodils in April, tulips in May.

Some of us, on the other hand, are darkness-lovers. We do

not dislike the early and late daylight of June, whippoorwill's graytime, but we cherish the gradually increasing dark of November, which we wrap around ourselves in the prosperous warmth of woodstove, oil, electric blanket, storm window, and insulation. We are partly tuber, partly bear. Inside our warmth we fold ourselves in the dark and its cold—around us, outside us, safely away from us; we tuck ourselves up in the long sleep and comfort of cold's opposite, warming ourselves by thought of the cold, lighting ourselves by darkness's idea. Or we are Persephone gone underground again, cozy in the amenities of Hell. Sheltered between stove and electric light, we hollow islands of safety within the cold and dark. As light grows less each day, our fur grows thicker. By December 22 we are cozy as a cat hunkered under a Glenwood.

Often October has shown one snow flurry, sometimes even September. For that matter, it once snowed in New Hampshire every month of the year. In 1816 it snowed and froze in June, in July, in August—the Poverty Year, season of continuous Winter, when farmers planted over and over again, over and over again ripped out frozen shoots of corn and pumpkin. An 1815 volcanic eruption in Indonesia did it—though at the time our preachers thought the source more local and divine wrath explicit.

Winter starts in November, whatever the calendar says, with gray of granite, with russet and brown of used leaves. In November stillness our stonewalls wait, attentive, and gaunt revenant trunks of maple and oak settle down for Winter's stasis, which annually mimics and presages death for each of us and for the planet. November's palette, Braque's analytic cubism, squared with fieldstones, interrupts itself briefly with the bright-flapped caps of deer hunters and their orange jackets. Always it is modified by the black-green fir, enduring, hinting at permanence. Serious snow begins one November afternoon. South of us Mount Kearsarge gradually disappears into white gauzy cloud, vanishing mountain, weather-sign for all of us to its north. For one hundred and eighty years the

people of this house have looked south at dawn's light and
again at sunset to tell the coming weather, reliable in 1803
when the first builder put in the south windows and reliable
still. When Kearsarge disappears the storm comes closer. Birds
gather at the feeder, squabbling, gobbling their weight. When
they are full they look for shelter, and we do the same, or at
least we bring wood from the shed to stack beside the old Glen-
woods and the new Jøtul.

Every year the first snow sets me dreaming. By March it will
only bring the grumps, but November snow is revenance, a
dreamy restitution of childhood or even infancy. Tighten the
door and settle a cloth snake against the breeze from the door's
bottom; make sure the storms are firmly shut; add logs to the
stove and widen the draft. Sit in a chair looking south into
blue twilight that arrives earlier every day—as the sky flakes
and densens, as the first clear flakes float past the porch's wood
to light on dirt of the driveway and on brown frozen grass or
dry stalks of the flower border. They seem tentative and awk-
ward at first, then in a hastening host a whole brief army falls,
white militia paratrooping out of the close sky over various
textures, making them one. Snow is white and gray, part and
whole, infinitely various yet infinitely repetitious, soft and
hard, frozen and melting, a creaking underfoot and a sound-
lessness. But first of all it is the reversion of many into one. It
is substance, almost the idea of substance, that turns grass,
driveway, hayfield, old garden, log pile, Saab, watering
trough, collapsed barn, and stonewall into the one white.
We finish early in November the task of preparing the house
for snow—tacking poly over the low clapboards, raking leaves
against the foundations as high as we can rake them. When
the first real snow arrives, no dusting half inch but a solid foot,
we complete the insulation, for it is snow that keeps us warm.
After a neighbor's four-wheel-drive pick-up, plough bolted in
front, swoops clean our U-shaped driveway, and after we dig
out the mailbox for Bert's rural delivery, it is time to heap the

snow over leaves and against poly, around the house, on all sides of the house, against the granite foundation stones. Arctic winds halt before this white guard. When bright noon melts inches of snow away from the house, reflecting heat from the snowy clapboard, it leaves cracks of cold air for us to fill when new snow falls all Winter long.

But November, although it begins Winter, is only Winter's approach, with little snow and with cold that announces itself only to increase. The calendar's Winter begins at the solstice, Advent's event: the birth of the child who rises from Winter to die and rise again in Spring. November is Autumn's burial, and the smoke of victims sacrificed is thanks for harvest and magic as we go into ourselves like maples for Winter's bear-sleep. We make transition by way of feast and anticipatory snow, toward the long, white, hard hundred days, the true Winter of our annual deaths. We wait for December to feel the *cold*, I mean COLD, for longer than a week, but now we are ready for snow.

The first big snow accumulates one night. Kearsarge may disappear at noon, and darkness start early. In teatime twilight, big flakes slowly, as if hesitant, reel past the empty trees like small white leaves, star-shaped and infrequent. By bedtime, driveway and lawn turn shaggy with the first cover. It is good to go to bed early in Winter, and tonight as we sleep our dreams take punctuation from the thudding of snowploughs as they roll and bluster up and down Route 4, shaking the house yet comforting our sleep: Someone takes care, the solitary captains in their great snowships breasting through vast whiteness, cleaving it sideways into gutter drifts. If we stir as they thump past, we watch revolving yellow lights flash through our windows and reflect on the ceiling. We roll over and fall back into protected sleep. In a house full of pets we sleep not alone, for the snowploughs that reassure us frighten our dog like thunder or riflefire; cats crawl between our warm bodies under warmer electric blankets.

When we become aware, by the ploughs' repeated patrols, that the first deep snow accumulates, when the first intense and almost unbreakable sleep finishes and we climb to the frangible second storey of the night's house, I pull myself out of bed at two or three in the morning to inspect the true oncoming of Winter's work. I walk through the dark house from one vantage to another—parlor window that looks west toward pond, kitchen from which I look toward Kearsarge, dining room that gives on the north and, if I twist, back to the slopes of Ragged Mountain rising east above us. The night's flaking air breaks black sky into white flecks, silent and pervasive, shuttering the day's vista. This snow fills the air and the eyes, the way on Spring nights peepers fill the ears. Everywhere I look, limited by snow-limits, cold dewy whiteness takes everything into itself. Beside the covered woodshed, side by side, I see the shapes of two small cars rounded and smooth like enormous loaves of dead-white bread. Where the woodpile waits for final stacking in the shed, a mound rises with irregular sticks jagging out of it. Up on the hill the great cowbarn labors under a two-foot layer of snow, its unpainted vertical boards a dark upright shadow in all the whiteness, like the hemlocks above it on Ragged's hill. Although snowploughs keep Route 4 passable, they do not yet scrape to the macadam: In the darkness the highway is as white as the hayfields on either side. Down the road the white cottage disappears against the white field, its green shutters a patch of vacancy in the whiteness. In the stillness of two A.M., in a silent unlit moment with no ploughs thudding, I regard a landscape reverted to other years by the same snow, and I might be my great-grandfather gazing from the same windows in 1885. Or it might be his mother's eyes I gaze from, born on a Wilmot hill in 1789. Or maybe I look, centuries earlier, from the eyes of a Penacook wintering over the pond.

But now the snowplough's thunder signals itself, and I watch the revolving yellow light reflect upward into white prodigious air, and hear the great bruising barge roar and rumble past the house as a steel prow swooshes high waves of whiteness up and over the gutter almost to the front of the house, and buries the mailbox.

One year the first great snow came Christmas Eve after the family had struggled to bed. When we lit the tree in the morning, the day past the windows was thick and dark, and as we opened our presents the snow deepened in yard and hayfield outside, and on Christmas Day, all day, the great ploughs of state and town kept Route 4 clear. Snow stopped at three in the afternoon, and when Forrest rolled in to plough the driveway in the early blue twilight, Jane heaped slices of turkey between homemade bread to comfort him in his cab as he drove over the countryside digging people out.

The next morning was cold, thirty below, cold enough to notice. January in fact is the coldest month, although many would argue for February. Usually our cold is dry and does not penetrate so much as damp cold. December of 1975, our first full Winter here, I tried starting the Plymouth one morning with normal confidence in the old six and without cold-weather precautions; I flooded it. When I looked at the thermometer I was astonished to find it seventeen degrees below zero, for my face and forehead had not warned me that it was *cold*. I had recently spent my winters in Michigan's damp cold; Ann Arbor's occasional zero felt harsher than New Hampshire's common twenty below.

Later that Winter we did not complain of mildness. In January of 1976, morning after morning was thirty below; one morning on the porch the thermometer read thirty-eight degrees under—a temperature we did not equal until 1984. My grandmother had just died at ninety-seven, and she had spent most of her late Winters going south to Connecticut. The house had grown unaccustomed to Winter, the old heavy wooden storm windows broken, no central heat, and no insulation. Jane and I had never lived without central heat. Now we had a parlor Glenwood stove for heating, two kerosene burners in the kitchen, and on occasion an electric oven with the door open. This twelve-room house, in January of 1976, dwindled to a one-room house with a kitchen sometimes habitable. Working at the dining room table twenty feet from the living room's Glenwood I felt chilly. At the time we were too excited or triumphant to complain: We were camping out; we were earning our stripes. The next summer we added aluminum combination storms and screens together with some insulation; we added two more woodstoves, one for each study, so that we could each work despite the Winter. (My grandparents survived with only two woodstoves because they bustled around all day; in our work we sit on our duffs and require extra stoves.) When February came we learned we had passed our initiation, for it had been the coldest January since New Hampshire started keeping records more than a hundred years earlier. In all my grandmother's ninety-seven Januarys she had not known so cold a month.

My grandfather Wesley Wells worked all day without any heat except for the bodies of his cows. While he sat at morning and evening between two great steaming black and white Holstein hulks, pulling the pale thin tonnage of blue milk from their cud-chewing bodies, he kept warm. Other chores were cold. I can remember him, on my Winter visits to the farm as a boy, scurrying into the house for a warm-up between his outdoor tasks, rubbing his hands together, opening the drafts of one of the woodstoves and looming over it for a moment. Early and late, he moved among cold sheds and unheated barns. In the cowbarn, he fed the cattle hay, grain, and ensilage, and provided his horse Riley with oats and hay and water. He let the Holsteins loose to wander stiff-legged to the old cement watering trough next to the milk room, from which he first removed a layer of ice. Their muzzles dipped one by one into the near-freezing water. And he fed the sheep in sheepbarn and sheepyard. From the sheep's trough he scooped water for the hens who lived next door to the sheep, and he carried feed for his hens from the grainshed beside the cowbarn.

He would start these chores early, most days of deep Winter, rising at four-thirty, perhaps three hours before the sun, to do half the daily chores of feeding and watering, of milking and readying milk for the milktruck, because the special daily chores of Winter were the year's hardest, the pains of minus twenty exacerbated by hard labor. To chop wood for next year's stove, the farmer stalked with his ax into his woodlot after chores and breakfast, and often marched far enough so that he carried with him his bread and butter, meat, pie, and thermos of coffee for dinner. Setting out with a great ax, usually working alone, the farmer chopped a tree down, trimmed branches, cut the trunk into four-foot sections, and stacked it. Later he would hitch oxen to the sledge and fetch the cordwood downhill to the barnyard for cutting to stove-length pieces and for splitting. Maybe ten cord of a Winter for the house—more for the sugaring in March.

In January he harvested another Winter crop, the crop that people forget when they think of the needs of an old farm—the harvest of ice, cut in great oblongs two or three feet thick from Eagle Pond, ox-sledded up to the icehouse in back of the cowbarn's watering trough, packed against warm weather six months hence. Each Winter the farmer waited for a cold stretch, augering through the pond ice to check its thickness. Then he cut checkerboard squares with an ice saw. He kept himself heavily mittened not only against cold and wind rattling over the open desert lake, but also against the inevitable clasp of near-frozen water. A crew of them—neighbors cooperated to fetch ice—sawed and grappled, lifted and hauled, hard work and cold work. In the icehouse they stacked layers of ice, thickly insulated with sawdust, to last from the earliest warmth of April through hot spells of June and the long Summer hay days of July and August through Autumn with its Indian Summer, until the pond froze again. In the hot months my grandfather brought one chunk a day downhill from the icehouse, great square balanced with ice tongs on his shoulder, to the toolshed behind the kitchen where my grandmother kept her icebox, drip drip. Most ice went to cool the milk, hot from the udders of Holsteins, so that it would not spoil overnight in Summer. July and August, I was amazed every time we dug through the wet sawdust in the cool shade of the icehouse to find cold Winter again—packed silvery slab of Eagle Pond preserved against Summer, just as we hayed to preserve Summer's grass for the Winter cattle. On the hottest days when we returned sweaty from haying, my grandfather cracked off a little triangle of ice for me to suck on. Every January when he dug down in the icehouse to bury his crop of new ice, he found old ice underneath. After all, you never wanted to find yourself all out; some years, there might be hot days even in November when you would require a touch of ice. One long hot Autumn he found at the bottom of the icehouse, farther than he ever remembered digging, a small coffin-shaped remnant from times past, ice that might have been five years old, he told me, maybe older.

And my grandfather told me how, in the state of Maine especially, in the old days, sailing ships loaded ice and sawdust in Winter and sailed this cargo—transient mineral, annual and reproducible reverse-coal tonnage—down the East Coast to unload its cool for the South, which never otherwise saw a piece of ice: ice by the ton for coastal cities like Charleston, South Carolina. Sometimes they sailed all the way to the West Indies with their perishable glossy cargo: Maine ice for the juleps of Charleston, northern January cooling Jamaica's rum.

By tradition, the hard snow and heavy cold of January take a vacation for the eldritch out-of-time phenomenon of January thaw. Sometimes the January thaw comes in February, sometimes it never arrives at all, and on the rarest occasions it starts early and lasts all Winter. Mostly the January thaw lives up to its name. Some strange day, after a week when we dress in the black of twenty below, we notice that we do not back up to the fire as we change our clothing. Extraordinary. Or at midday we pick up the mail in our shirtsleeves, balmy at forty-two degrees. (It is commonplace to observe that a temperature which felt Arctic late in August feels tropical in mid-January.) Icicles drip, snow slides off the south roof in midday sun, and mud takes over the driveway. Snow melts deeply away from clapboard and poly. Or the January thaw comes with warm rain ("If this was snow we'd have twelve feet . . ."), and if warm rain pours for three January days, as I have known it to do, Ragged's melt floods our driveway, snow vanishes from all hayfields, and water drowns the black ice of Eagle Pond. Our small universe confuses itself with false Spring. Bears wake perplexed and wander looking for deer corpses or compost heaps, thinking that it's time to get on with it. I remember fetching the newspaper one morning at five-thirty (I pick up the *Globe* outside a store that does not open for customers, slugabeds, until six o'clock) on the third day of a warm rain. Chugging through deep mud in my outboard

Nissan, I pulled up at the wet porch to see a huge white cat rooting about in perennials beside the walk, a white pussycat with black spots ... Oh, no. I remained in the front seat quietly reading the paper, careful not to make a startling sound or otherwise appear rude until the skunk wandered away.

Until we replaced rotten sills three years ago, a family of skunks lived in our rootcellar every Winter. We never saw them but we found their scat; we found the holes by which they entered and exited. Of course we confirmed their presence by another sense. In the Spring they sometimes quarreled, possibly over the correct time and place for love, and we could hear them arguing and discovered that skunks used on each other their special skunk equipment: Once a year in February or March we needed to throw all windows open. On one occasion, Ann Arbor friends visited in March, dear friends notable for an immaculate house in a culture of unspotted houses. When we brought them home with their skis from the airport, we opened the door to discover that our rootcellar family had suffered domestic disagreement. We opened all downstairs windows although it was fifteen below; as we prepared to take our friends up to their bedroom, where the air would be purer, we opened the hallway door to discover a dead rat on the carpet, courtesy of a guardian cat. Welcome to the country.

January thaw is dazzling but it lasts only a moment. If this were January in England we would expect crocuses and snowdrops soon; here we know enough to expect replacement battalions of snow's troopers following on coldness that freezes the melt, covering it with foot upon foot of furry whiteness and moon-coldness. We return to the satisfactions of Winter, maybe even to the deliverance and delirium of a full moon. In New Hampshire the full moon is remarkable all year long because we suffer relatively little from garbage-air and less from background light. The great cloudless night of the full moon is werewolf time, glory of silver-pale hauntedness whenever it happens but most beautiful in Winter. I set the internal alarm, maybe three or four nights in a row, and wander, self-made ghost, through pale rooms in the pewter light while the moon magnifies itself in bright hayfields and reflects upward, a sun from middle earth, onto shadowy low ceilings. High sailing above, higher than it has a right to, bigger, the February full moon, huge disc of cold, rides and slides among tatters of cloud. My breathing speeds, my pulse quickens; for half an hour I wander, pulled like a tide through the still house in the salty half light, more asleep than awake, asleep not in house or nightshirt but in moon, moon, moon . . . What old animal awakens and stretches inside the marrow of the bones? What howls? What circles, sniffing for prey?

It's no Winter without an ice storm. When Robert Frost gazed at bowed-over birch trees and tried to think that boys had bent them playing, he knew better: "Ice-storms do that." They do that and a lot more, trimming disease and weakness out of the tree—the old tree's friend, as pneumonia used to be the old man's. Some of us provide life-support systems for our precious shrubs, boarding them over against the ice, for the ice storm takes the young or unlucky branch or birch as well as the rotten or feeble. One February morning we look out our windows over yards and fields littered with kindling, small twigs and great branches. We look out at a world turned into one diamond, ten thousand carats in the line of sight, twice as many facets. What a dazzle of spinning refracted light, spiderwebs of cold brilliance attacking our eyeballs! All Winter we wear sunglasses to drive, more than we do in Summer, and never so much as after an ice storm, with its painful glaze reflecting from maple and birch, granite boulder and stonewall, turning electric wires into bright silver filaments. The snow itself takes on a crust of ice, like the finish of a clay pot, that carries our weight and sends us swooping and sliding. It's worth your life to go for the mail. Until sand and salt redeem the highway, Route 4 is quiet. We cancel the appointment with the dentist, stay home, and marvel at the altered universe, knowing that midday sun will strip ice from tree and roof and restore our ordinary white Winter world.

·   ·   ·

Another inescapable attribute of Winter, increasing in years of affluence, is the ski people, cold counterpart to the Summer folks who fill New Hampshire's Julys and Augusts. Now the roads north from Boston are as dense on a February Friday as they are on a July, and late Sunday afternoon, southbound Interstate 93 backs up miles from the tollbooth. On innumerable Toyotas pairs of skis ride north and south every Winter weekend; at Christmas vacation and school holidays every hotel room fills all week with families of flatlanders. They wait in line at the tows, resplendent in the costumes of money, booted and coifed in bright petrochemical armor. They ride, they swoop, they fall, they drink whiskey, and the bonesetter takes no holiday on a New Hampshire February weekend, and the renter of crutches earns time and a half. Now that cross-country rivals downhill, the ski people grow older and more various. Tourism, which rivals the yard sale as the major north country industry, brings Massachusetts and New York money to fatten purses in the cold country. In the fashionable areas—much of Vermont and Waterville Valley in New Hampshire's White Mountains—restaurants and boutiques, cute-shops and quiche-cafés buzz like Winter's blackflies.

Few natives ski, though some have always done, and in our attic there are wide heavy wooden skis from the time of the Great War on which my mother and her sisters traipsed all Winter, largely doing cross-country but perfectly willing to slide down a hill. Old-timers remember the horse-as-ski-tow, pulling adventurers uphill.

The motorcycle roar of snowmachines, from a distance indistinguishable from chainsaws, interrupts the downy quiet of midweek evenings, as kids roar along disused railroad tracks and over the surface of frozen lakes. Older folks, men mostly, park their bobhouses on frozen Winter lakes, saw holes through the ice, light a fire, warm themselves with a pint of whiskey, and fish for the wormless perch of Winter. Like deer hunting in November, this fishing is not mere sport; it fills the freezers of shacks, trailers, and extended farmhouses. On Eagle Pond we count six or a dozen bobhouses each Winter, laboriously translated by pick-up and slipped across the ice to a lucky spot.

After the labor of cordwood and ice in the old days, as the Winter ended, followed the great chore of maplesugaring. It still arrives, though without so much labor. Usually it comes in one stretch of March, but on occasion the conditions for sap turn right for two weeks in February, go wrong for twenty days, then right themselves again—a split season for sugaring. Right conditions are warm days when snow melts followed by cold nights when it freezes.

Nowadays people suction sap from the sugarbush with miles of plastic tubing. In the old time, syrupers pounded the spigot into the tree—several of them in a good-sized three-hundred-year-old maple—and hung a bucket from each for the sap to drip into. My grandfather trudged from tree to tree every day, wearing a wooden yoke across his shoulders; long pails hung from the ends of it, narrow on top and wide on bottom, for collecting sap from each bucket. He emptied these yoke pails into a great receptacle sledged by an ox—oxen were especially useful in the Winter, slow but unbothered by snow—and when he filled this great sledge kettle, his ox pulled it to a funnel and pipe whence the sap flowed downhill to a storage tank behind the saphouse. Gathering sap was a third of the work, or maybe a quarter. There was cordwood to cut, to burn under the trays boiling the sap down. Someone tended the fire day and night, watched and tested the sap on its delicate journey to syrup. In 1913 my grandfather corked five hundred gallons at a dollar a gallon, big money in 1913, with the help of his father-in-law Ben Keneston, cousin Freeman, and Anson the hired man. Remember that it takes about forty gallons of sap, boiled down, to make a gallon of syrup.

Not only the cash was sweet. To maplesyrup and maplesugar my grandfather and grandmother added honey from the beehive beside the barn and the hollyhocks; they grew and produced their own sweetening. But big money from syrup bought land and paid taxes. Often their tax was little or nothing, for in the old days many farmers paid their taxes by doing road work—scraping and rolling the dirt roads, filling in with hardpan, and in Winter rolling down the snow of the road to make it fit for the runners of sleighs, taking on a mile of Wilmot's Grafton Turnpike.

March was always the month for blizzards. Still is. It is the time when we all tell ourselves: *We've had enough of Winter.* Old folks come back from Florida and Hilton Head; younger ones, fed up, head off for a week where the weather performs like May or June in New Hampshire. Every morning the *Globe* measures a word from Florida: *baseball* . . . In New Hampshire, tantalizing melt is overwhelmed by four feet of snow, drifts to twelve feet . . . We comfort each other, when we use the form of complaint for our boasting, that even if we lost the old outhouse yesterday or the '53 Buick that the chickens use for Summer roosting, what comes quick in March goes quick in March, and three or four days from now it'll melt to reveal the lost Atlantis of the family barnyard. Then three or four days later we wake to another four feet.

In the 1940s, the old people still bragged about the great blizzard of '88. My Connecticut grandfather and my New Hampshire one, who shared little, shared the blizzard of '88: a great watershed for bragging or for telling lies about. And in the 1980s I still ask old people what they remember that *their* old people told them about '88, much as the '88ers themselves asked their old-timers about the Poverty Year of 1816. Paul Fenton told me a story he heard as a boy, not about '88 but just about "the big snows we used to have, back in the old days." It seems that a bunch went out after a heavy snow, dragging the roads with the help of oxen so that people could use their sleighs and sledges, when one of the oxen slipped and got stuck, couldn't move at all, got a hoof caught in something . . . Well, they dug down, dug around, trying to free the ox's hoof, and what do you know . . . That ox had stuck its foot into a chimney!

Now, the blue snow of 1933 is *not* a lie. I am sure of it because of the way Ansel Powers tells me about it, because his wife Edna confirms it, because Les Ford from Potter Place, who has never been known to collaborate on a story, remembers it just as well and tells the same stories. It may be hard to believe, *but it was blue*. You stuck a shovel in it and it was *blue*, blue as that sky, blue as a bachelor's-button. It fell in April, a late snow, and it fell fast. Les remembers that he'd been to a dance at Danbury, and when he went to bed at midnight, the sky was clear and full of stars; when he woke up in the morning, there it was. The snowploughs were disassembled for Summer; the road agent had to start up the old dozer and go patrol the road with it to clear a way for Model T's—and a few shiny Model A's. Sam Duby, the same blacksmith who made the first snowploughs in Andover, woke up at two or three in the morning and had to do something, you know. Well, the outhouse was across the road in the barn and he went out to the end of the porch and it was snowing to beat the band and he just dropped a load right there . . . He's the only one who saw it snow; the rest of us went to bed under stars, woke up to the sun shining on three feet of blue snow.

In *The Voyage of the Beagle* Charles Darwin wrote about finding red snow, *Protococcus nivalis*, on the Peuquenes Ridge in Chile in 1835. "A little rubbed on paper gives it a faint rose tinge mingled with a little brick-red." When he examined it later, Darwin found "microscopical plants." As far as I know, no one took our blue snow into a laboratory.

Of course it snows in April every year, most often white, but you cannot call it Winter anymore. Snow sticks around, in the north shade, most years until early in May, but it is ragged and dirty stuff, and we overlook it as we gaze in hopeful amazement at this year's crop of daffodils. Every year the earlier daffodils fill with snow, bright yellow spilling out white crystals, outraged optimism overcome by fact, emblem of corny desolation. And the worst storm I have driven through, after ten New Hampshire Winters, occurred a few years back on the ninth day of May.

But annual aberration aside, March is the end of Winter, and the transition to Spring is April's melt. One year not long ago we had an open Winter, with very little snow, *no* snow we all said; we exaggerated a little, for we had an inch here and an inch there. The Winter was not only dry but mild, which was a good thing, for an open Winter with cold weather destroys flowers and bushes and even trees, since snow is our great insulator. As it was, in our open Winter we suffered one cold patch—twenty below for a week—and in the Spring that followed, and in the Summer, we discovered winterkill: A few rosebushes and old lilacs, plants and bulbs that had survived for decades, didn't make it that year. When Spring came without a melt, when mild days softened with buttery air and the protected daffodils rose blowing yellow trumpets, we felt uneasy. All of us knew: Lacking the pains of Winter, we did not deserve the rapture and the respite of Spring.

Our annual melt is the wild, messy, glorious loosening of everything tight. It is gravity's ecstasy, as water seeks its own level on every level, and the noise of water running fills day and night. Down Ragged Mountain the streams rush, cutting through ice and snow, peeling away Winter's cold layers: rush, trickle, rush. Busy water moves all day and all night, never tired, cutting away the corrupt detritus of Winter; fingers of bare earth extend down hillsides; south sides of trees extend bare patches, farther every day; root-pattern rivulets, melting, gather downhill to form brief streams; dirt roads slog and driveways turn swamps.

Then it dries; last snow melts; trees bud green; soft air turns. Who can believe in Winter now?

All of us. We know that Winter has only retreated, waiting. When the bear comes out of its Winter sleep, Winter itself goes into hibernation, sleeping off the balmy months of peepersing until the red leaf wakes it again and the white season returns with the New Hampshire Winter by which we know ourselves.

Spring

Spring

Spring is the least of our seasons, and it has built no constituency in New Hampshire. Our countryside attracts leaf people in Autumn who gape with good reason at the fauve hillsides; Winter's skiers who drive north from Boston, skies atop Audis, and whole families over Christmas and schoolbreaks who break rich ankles; uncountable Summer people who laze a permitted annual dally on the shore or in sailboats or simply in sun and play bridge at night by the light of state-liquor-store gin. But New Hampshire's Spring people distinguish themselves by nonexistence. In April our restaurants and motels close for the month as weary industrialists of tourism take holiday in Carolina, Georgia, or Florida. For motelers and maitre-d's, Spring floats a brief intermission between the anxieties of ski time, when everything glides on the temperature, and the certain labors of long Summer. Real Spring people, often identical to our own Summer people, gather at Hilton Head or sniff the sweet air of Savannah. Spring is long, tender, and luxurious in the Southeast, where the crocus shoves up its head in January and the flowering shrubs, like rhododendrons at the Masters in Augusta, waft rich odoriferous air through the warm nights.

Of the world's seasons Spring has the best press. Where are the songs of Spring? Everyplace. It is when the voice of the turtle is heard in the land. A later poet told how a young man's fancy lightly turned; another called April the cruelest month; another claimed always to mourn with ever-returning Spring; still another, resident of Italy, protested, "Oh, to be in England now that April's there."

Now I have never spent a whole Spring in Carolina or Georgia, only flown in for a brief hallucinatory visit from chill muddy April or pestiferous May to hover a moment in the saccharine air of Milledgeville, Macon, or Charlotte. But in England I have spent four Springs; I count them as a miser counts gold: two at Oxford, two in a village called Thaxted, not far from Cambridge. In England sometimes a January day can be purest Spring: warm, muddy, lazy, sunny, with crocuses starting up. Correspondingly, in weird Albion, a gale always whoops out of the northeast early in August after a warmish week, gritty wind thrashes rain through the Doctor's Garden Fete, and somebody says, "It was rather a short Summer but quite a nice one . . ."

But in England April, May, and early June are lemony days of velvet-green grass in the Fellows' Garden with bowls and croquet; evenings lengthening like the promise of an afterlife; balls at the colleges that end with a group photograph in the quadrangle at six in pale dawn; ten million daffodils by the Cam at the backs of the Cambridge colleges; and at Oxford the year's climax is Eights Week, early in June. The eights are crews competing on the Isis, but never mind. Pubs stay open, girls bloom into English roses, promise gilds itself in the golden sun of arrogant youth brazen with promise, the sun never sets, the sky never clouds, strawberries and champagne endlessly arrive carried by dutiful and conservative servants who know their places. We know: The beastly Huns, not to mention the Irish and the Working Classes, will never disturb our tranquil luxury.

·   ·   ·

In New Hampshire Spring begins with rain and melt. For that matter, it continues to snow, at least from time to time, late in March through April. Spring snow rattles Winter's death— or is it the triumphant final tour of Winter? Well, *almost* final: perhaps *one* more go at Hedda, for charity of course. Or Winter returns like a forty-four-year-old relief pitcher who has been practicing a knuckler in the backyard, throwing it to his moth- er. Now we become impatient: Let us give Winter its gold watch; let us award it an honorary Oscar or a day of its own at Cooperstown; let us push it off to a condominium in the keys of Antarctica and stop all this damned nonsense about a comeback.

Water begins it, warm rain over the wasted gray drifts of March. Long days and nights of rain wear dingy ruts in our snowfields, or warm days of early sun release meltwater from crystals of hill and meadow, and the great crashing melt dozes creeks and streams, raising instant rivers where Summer's gulch is dry. Water is never lazy, never quiet; it talks all day and gossips all night, chattering down hills through gullies to ditches at roadside. On the ponds ice rots and gray stains spread over level white. Provident ice fishermen have removed their bobhouses by early March, but every Spring on New Hampshire's lakes some of these shacks tilt and sag and tumble through cold water to lake bottom. How many small huts, like outhouses *d'antan*, rot on pond bottoms? Ice leaves the lake one day when we do not notice; for weeks it has crept out from the shoreline, frayed from its muddy border, but when we gaze from the bridge to the pond's center, the ice looks steady and unbroken still. Then it is suddenly gone, for it sinks to the bot- tom while we are never looking.

Now pond and lake swell, rise, widen over meadow and bogland, lift picnic tables from the old year's Summer and carry them a rod like pranksters, or misplace canoes, rafts, and docks improperly secured. Birch and popple that start at the water's edge now loom from water itself. Long ago our market town of Franklin routinely flooded in Spring, the Pem-

igewasset widening and lifting into low-set workers' housing
near the mills. Now a dam constructed by Army engineers in
1940 backs the water into a valley near the town of Hill.

During wet, melt, and high water, beavers chew at anything
arboreal that appears attractive. At the south end of Eagle
Pond they populate a boggy place and make it boggier with
dams; nearby groves prickle with cone-shaped pointy stumps.
Sometimes they leave behind a tree they've chewed down if
it's too big to pull, or maybe they only wanted to strip bark off.
There's a worked-over beaver plantation near the house at the
north end of the hayfield between Route 4 and the railroad.
These must be tasty trees, popple and gray birch, because the
creatures by-pass wood closer to their pond-home in order to
harvest this little grove. I've counted forty-seven chewed-off
stumps. The railroad trench cuts deeply below this patch,
and there's a rusty B & M fence to get through when the beaver
transports his timber to the pond. Near the fence a well-worn
trail looks like a cowpath or a lane trodden by habitual human
feet—except that this path goes under a strand of wire ten
inches off the ground. Here I've found a good-sized tree caught
in the fence, hanging a third of its length into the air over the
track; beavers are smart but they can't solve everything. Also
I've found a tree hauled a long way from its stump but caught
and wedged unmovable between other stumps. When I look at
the trail that the beavers wear by their haulage I'm dazzled:
After they roll the treetrunk down the sandbank, they must
carry it across tracks, up another bank, then down a steep slope
to Eagle Pond.

We never see beaver, except a distant nose sticking up from
the water, leaving a V behind it as it swims across the pond
carrying a stick. When we first moved here a cousin came to
the kitchen door asking permission to trap beaver on our land.
I signed the paper out of family feeling and cowardice, but I
felt sorry for Bucky. It took six months before rage took guilt's
place: I wanted to advance my cousin capital for more traps.
Beaver chewed down four birches by our swimming place

and let them rot; elsewhere they flooded gardens and hayfields by building dams. The fish and game people spend half their working hours blowing up beaver dams with dynamite. Lately the price for pelts has dropped like a chewed popple and my cousin has stopped trapping and beaver multiply.

As the air warms, houseflies wake from their Winter sleep and congregate at upstairs windows. For a week of this weather houseflies are the only pest, unless the driveway is a pest, for it becomes momentarily impassable, scourge of transmissions. Mud season's yellow viscosity churns under struggling wheels without exhausting itself to a solid bottom. We stay off the dirt roads that climb Ragged and circle the pond. Bert the RD lets air out of his tires for traction but gets stuck in mud season as he never sticks in blizzards or ice storms; it is the worst driving and the worst walking of the year. Sometimes the mud freezes at night, a grid of frozen sea-ways, torture for the shocks of cars; then by noon it melts back to colloid obscenity.

Sometimes this condition lasts for weeks but usually it is quick, and when it dries the air warms and the light turns yellowish, as if the mud's churn buttered the air. For a few days we enjoy the classic look of high Spring. Crocuses stick their heads up opening fragile tentative mouths; daffodils climb beginning to unfold; the tulip rises with promise of outrage. Jane casts off Winter gloom and works at the garden in a frenzy—swooping away gray leaves matted over the borders and against the house, raking twigs broken off by ice and gravel shoved everywhere by the snowplough. Jane frees soil for the grandeur of crack and blossom, enabling flowers. She works in such a frenzy for good reason: One day when the sun passes Ragged's edge and warms the air midmorning, suddenly *the blackflies are among us.*

For a day or two they don't bite. Then they start biting. Our Egyptian plague, blackflies annually destroy New Hampshire's Spring. A bumper sticker turns up, NUKE THE BLACK FLIES, but drastic as the suggestion may be, it's pointless: After the last war only blackflies will prove nasty enough to survive, to evolve over a million years their own malicious culture. Oh, they bite. You hardly see them (no-see-ums is one of their names) but they have been with us forever. As Parkman describes it, in the seventeenth century—and doubtless ever since they wandered this way from the Bering Strait—Indians lived in teepees dense with smoke to discourage blackflies and mosquitoes.

In New Hampshire although the air is balmy now we wear armor outdoors: long thick socks rolled up over heavy jeans, gloves, long sleeves rolled down, and for many a beekeeper's mask and hat. Otherwise flies get in our hair and smuggle themselves into the house. We don't always feel them hit but we know afterward: Great red welts rise on our skin. My mother-in-law was once bitten between her eyes so that her two eyes shut. Dogs go raw on their bald bellies.

We dab dope on face, neck, hair, hands, wrists, and ankles; it helps, if we keep on doing it, but it does not satisfy. Blackflies buzz around us forming an angry mobile helmet; they swarm and wheel within half an inch of our faces. Sometimes in Spring I umpire softball games at the village school in Danbury, making crazy signals as my hands flip in constant involuntary motion warding blackflies. Similar wild signs emanate from pitcher, batter, and outfielders. It is spastic baseball, and if we were major leaguers we would be signaling—*Take! Hit! Steal! Bunt! Run! Don't run!*—on every pitch.

Mostly we stay inside. Jane makes desperate forays into her garden, transplanting this, fertilizing that, watering hastily; then she comes inside and takes a shower. Meantime tulips rise in their splendor, and daffodils that couldn't care less about blackflies dance their yellow dance on the granity hill behind the house. By the playhouse my cousin Freeman built for my grandmother Kate when she was five in 1880, with a noble slab of glacier-granite beside it, the ten thousand (really about two hundred) golden or gold and white daffodils raise bright agreeable faces. Uphill by the barn, and beside the woodshed under a sugarmaple near another boulder, and at the margin of the hayfield that runs south toward Kearsarge, Jane's daffodil armies march, onward floral soldiers. Oh, most wonderful of flowers, sun-colored welcoming the sun, vigorous handsome energetic golden trumpets of Spring heralding Summer! I stare at them dreamily all day, happy to accept their wild generosity, safe behind panes of glass.

When blackflies start to diminish mosquitoes arrive, and Spring is the least of our seasons. Here we don't suffer quite so much from mosquitoes; they are not so numerous as blackflies: As if to compensate for their numbers, of course, one mosquito can wreak havoc on a picnic or a night's sleep. But now I have gone on into Summer. Fair enough: So do the blackflies.

The first vegetable to plant is peas; we scatter the pale round seed on top of March's rags of snow. My mother remembers planting them regularly on Saint Patrick's Day, for peas like it damp and cold. When it warms in April and May the little bushes rise among blackflies, and covered with dope we pick fresh peas for the table late in June.

In the old days April and May were heavy farming times, made heavier by mud and flies. It was time to cart manure into cornfield and vegetable garden and plough it under. The big cowbarn that my great-grandfather built in 1865 still stands, south of the house a little above it. Huge blocks of granite shore its east side against Ragged's mudslide, blocks so huge you would swear cranes must have hauled them, not oxen. West the barn drops away downhill. Its main floor is the second storey, and as you look up from the house, the hill slopes enough so that there's a place to store a carriage under the grainshed that extends by the barnfloor. East of that door is the tie-up from which Holsteins strolled out to Ragged, which was their pasture, past the room for straining and cooling milk and the icehouse where we buried January's pond under sawdust for Summer. Over the cows hay lofted two storeys up.

And under the cows, west of the granite wall on bottom level, heaped the manure pile. Twice a day after milking we lifted long planks behind the cattle—rounded boards split from straight 1865 treetrunks, fastened to fixed floorboards by leather hinges made of worn-out harness—and slipped them over to open an eight-inch strip of lateral hole, the length of the tie-up. We scraped manure through this crack: Ranges of bovine excretion, down below, grew Alpine by April. For two weeks then—depending on snow, melt, and mud—my grandfather spent his days knee-deep in cowmanure. He kept a wagon for spreading it, which remained all year under the barn next to the manure pile, used every year for this one purpose only. The dump-cart remains there still, in good shape; if we wet the wheels to swell the wood tight inside iron rims, we could use it today. A small wooden seat rides on a spring next to a lever that lifted the truck bed up and slid manure off. The dump-cart under the barn flings its forearms down (arms that clutched the bony ribs of Riley and Roger, Ned's big bones, Nellie's black and Lady Ghost's pale gray) as if in despair on the humusy dirt of the floor where my grandfather let them fall in April of 1950. Beside it slope the diminishing Alps of manure from later that year, before his heart attack in November and the cows' December departure forever and ever. We use it still; it makes great topsoil.

He carted many loads to fertilize his fields. In the last decades of his life he did it alone, except for a few years when Anson came back, the hired man who had worked for them when my mother was a girl. He departed, one day in the 1920s, for twenty-five years. Anson suffered from a learning disability; in the old days we used a scientific term that we pronounced *mow*-ron. My grandfather wore boots and overalls, which hung on a hook under the barn, used only for this purpose, and with his shovel filled the cart and then drove it into the fields he planted with millet and fieldcorn and to the big garden plot. He spread it with the aid of gravity, and sometimes Anson, and with one shovel. When some was left over from the cropfields, he spread it on hayfields.

Mostly it was cowmanure. The horse's stall got dug out once or twice a week, horsemanure shoveled through a trap door down beside the Holsteins'. From the sheepbarn once or twice a year my grandfather extracted the rich mixture of sheepmanure and straw; my grandmother used some for her flowers. The crazy compost of the chickenhouse floor was too strong— chickenmanure, straw, and the decomposed detritus of all the garbage the hens had pecked at over the year: dry skeletal corn cobs, pale shreds of carrot tops and pea pods, even specks of old eggshells—and it would burn seed up.

There was even a little nightsoil, for my grandfather never quite accepted the indoor bathroom. In 1938 my grandparents added this innovation, struck off from the dining room: a narrow cold dingy miraculous toilet, washstand, and bathtub perpetually in trouble, water freezing in the Winter and spiders working their way up from bathtub drain all Summer. The bathroom supplemented but did not replace the outhouse. This old facility did not require a trudge through rain or snow. Although suitably far from living quarters, it situated itself under the continuous roof of the extended farmhouse. To reach it we exited the kitchen through the door to the toolshed, then through another door into the woodshed; we turned a corner at the back of the woodshed, and the outhouse door took the farthest corner. My grandfather, however, kept a roll of toilet paper near the cowmanure under the barn, and during chores if he was taken short he squatted there. I think he preferred the barn. Surely the notion of indoor defecation seemed obscene; even the outhouse was a little close to home. When he was old and sick he used the plumbing, I think with some distress.

When manure was spread on the fields, it was time to pull the plough from the long shed between chickencoop and sheepbarn where he stored plough, hayrack, mowing machine, and horsedrawn rake under cover from Winter weather. I suppose he ploughed five acres for garden, fieldcorn, and millet. I never knew my grandmother to buy a vegetable. Row after row of peas, beans in many varieties, bush beans and pole starring

Kentucky Wonders, beets, tomatoes, carrots, parsnips, potatoes, and Golden Bantam corn. Millet, or sometimes Hungarian, was sweet heavy-grained grass that he scythe-mowed every afternoon in July and August for his cattle; it helped to per-suade the cattle down from the hill's sweet grass for afternoon milking: Apparently millet and Hungarian were cow-delicious. (I tried them myself and they were sweet.) Field-corn, chopped up and siloed in September, provided nutriment for cattle all Winter long.

After ploughing when the time was right—usually after the last full moon around Memorial Day—it was time to plant. Soon enough it was time to weed, long hours with a hoe—my grandmother too—making sure that the vegetables started strong. No help from a Rototiller, but horse and harrow helped out between the spaced rows of corn.

Late Winter and early Spring was the time for new animals. Chicks were easiest. Before my time the hens hatched their own. At some point around the Great War the chicks began to come by parcel post, and in spring the P.O. down at Henry's store filled up with noisy rectangular boxes, cheep-cheep-cheep. Everybody kept chickens. We brought ours back to the shed and opened the boxes, each packed to sequester a hundred live chicks. Brooding factories packed the eggs before hatch-ing, and the tiny creatures cracked through their shells on their journey here, in the baggage cars of trains or in depots and post offices. The factories packed more than a hundred to be sure they delivered a hundred. Always a few eggs arrived unhatched and dead and one or two neonates lay stiff and dry among the riotous throng that rolled and teetered and chirped infant cries. We kept them warm and noisy in the shed until the nights were warmer; then they thrived in the yard behind the henhouse, a hundred new lives pecking into ancient dirt, eating grain from V-shaped feeders, drinking water I carried from the trough at roadside.

My grandfather bred his sheep so that lambs came in May after the mothers were out to pasture and the nights warm, but sometimes a lamb was born in the barn while it was still cold, which distressed him. New births every Spring were economically essential; sheep brought money disproportionate to the time they took, and twin lambs were a cause for rejoicing.

In the Winter the quantity of milk decreased rapidly as the great Holsteins swelled up with their babies, to dry out in the weeks before birth. Earlier when each cow came into heat, my grandfather left his bull alone with the chosen member of the black and white seraglio. Cedric Blasington, the farmer just down the road, lacked a bull himself; from time to time he led a distraught cow to our barn. My grandmother took her daughters up-attic to distract them while the service was performed, but they knew something was going on; they peeked to see cows jumping about in excitement. In Spring when the cows birthed my grandfather midwifed, tying a rope around the emerging calf to pull as the bossy pushed. Sometimes he had to enter a cow as far as he could reach to assist in a breech or posterior birth. One of the great sights on a farm is the joy of the Holstein sisterhood when a calf is born. Not only does the mother lick the child; the whole herd tries to, and the community celebrates, enormous black and white bovines leaping as much as they are able and bellowing out of their collective triumph.

When the first vegetables edge up from cracked mud and earth, the farmer's enemies assemble: weeds, drought or flood, slugs and cutworms, an entomologist's army of insects—and the imperturbable tribe of the woodchuck. Other pests include deer that browse a vegetable garden to devastation; chipmunks that eat the bulbs of flowers; bears that prefer the hives of the honeybee; foxes, weasels, fishers, and skunks that kill chickens; dogs and coyotes that kill sheep and lambs; and coons, shrewdest of vegetarian predators, that harvest our corn, taking the ripest ears on the morning before we boil water and walk into the cornpatch to pick supper.

Woodchucks are season-long, beginning in late Spring as soon as peas emerge, and do battle with the superiority of numbers, reinforcements, and stupidity. I don't suppose that my grandfather had much trouble from chucks until sometime in the 1920s when he understood that he could no longer keep a dog. A dog that runs loose eliminates the woodchuck problem; woodchucks have a dog problem. Hunter and Tripp herded sheep and helped find the cattle when they stayed up-mountain eating on late summer afternoons; they also protected vegetables and chickens from predators. But cars proliferated on Route 4 and got faster and faster until they reached speeds like 35 mph. At the north end of the farm a car approaches the house over a little ridge, unable to stop in time if the driver sees a creature in the road. The Model T killed Wesley's dogs. So my grandfather burying Tripp in his woe knew that the internal combustion engine forbade him the pleasure, companionship, and utility of dogs.

It would not have occurred to him to keep a pet inside and walk it on a leash. He loved his dogs; they earned their keep. Cats did too. The notion of a cat *indoors* made my grandmother wrinkle her nose—something she did frequently apropos rum, baseball on Sunday, ballroom dancing, and Frenchmen—although on rare occasions the senior barncat might be allowed entrance early in Autumn when frost chased fieldmice inside in numbers greater than traps could handle. Once the barncat ate improvident mice to its full, it was out on its ear.

The barn was dense with cats. Silage and grain encouraged rodent-presence, and without a resident cat-militia mice and rats would have eaten the grainshed hollow. My grandfather when he milked (like all farmer-grandfathers everywhere) swiveled a teat and squirted milk into the gaped jaws of kittens and cats who sat waiting for his performance, a little row of organic Staffordshire cats with pink mouths stretched wide. In the 1940s one old gray mother-tabby, shrewd about Route 4 and automobile behavior, teats hanging low from three-litter years, held perpetual sway, but her cleverness was an acquired characteristic, not transferable by Lamarckian genetics to her countless kittens. As a boy I buried one a week in the cats' graveyard between sheepbarn and vegetable garden.

Now we reverse old ways. Cats and dogs live indoors and our barns loom gray and silent without animals; I walk Gus along Route 4 on his chain; every day Jane and I drive or walk him to the triangular meadow by the pond or to a flattish stretch of New Canada Road or to cut-over acres of woodlot— someplace where cars are few and Gus can run loose. Ada guards the indoor house as Mio, Catto, Bella, and Amos did before them, performing effective duty against generations of mice, moles, voles, chipmunks—and one rat.

When we moved here a dozen years ago, we planted a garden that became a Woodchuck Resources Center. As a boy I would sit for an hour at dawn and another at dusk until I got a good shot at a woodchuck. My rifle was a short-barreled handmade old octagonal Mossberg .22 carbine, built for target shooting mostly. I practiced my eye by assassinating tin cans with my father and then when I was in my teens killed many woodchucks and buried them among the roadkilled kittens. But in my fifties I lack patience to sit for an hour waiting for the fat imbecilic figure of a woodchuck to stick its head out of its hole, sniff the air, and draw fire. Without patience, without a dog, our garden disappeared down woodchuck jaws year after year

—peas eaten down as they ripened, beets gnawed into the earth, Kentucky Wonders nipped in the bud. Old holes were rein-habited each year, and each year fresh sand heaped in fields near the garden reported growth in the chuck population. Suburban woodchucks from Massachusetts built second homes in New Hampshire. Five or six times a day I wandered across Route 4 swinging my elegant rifle, looking for a woodchuck to shoot. Usually I saw nothing; occasionally I shot from a distance and missed; once I killed a creature sunning himself behind the ruins of the sheepbarn.

Mostly they just ate us out. We tried folk remedies: dried blood, Kitty Litter, and planting marigolds. I bought one of the gas bombs Agway sells, but I wasn't sure how the subway system worked and I was wary of trying it. I raised a good fence, which helped, but I couldn't use an electric fence be-cause of the difficulties of stringing wire across Route 4. I stayed away from leg traps. On a visit to Agway, complaining about our woodchucks, I heard a story from a clerk: A year before, somebody had dropped around for one remedy and another, continually complaining and failing, getting madder and madder. He tried gas bombs and lost some chickens; he tried a leg trap and took a neighbor's shepherd to the vet with a broken leg. One day he arrived as red as the beets he had lost and bought sticks of dynamite and caps and went home and blew up his garden and hayfield. His garden was gone, his fields looked like Saipan—but he sure got that woodchuck.

Finally I bought a Hav-a-Heart trap, which Has its Heart by capturing the animal intact when he trips a pedal going after food. I baited it with vegetables and fruit and caught two or three woodchucks every Spring. These captures discouraged the tribe and allowed us three quarters of our garden. Of course the trap leaves the gardener with a problem: What do you do with the victim? Rumor suggests that some folks sneak live woodchucks by night into the gardens of local Democrats. I solved the problem my own way. When I caught Woody I took my Mossberg out of the closet and shot him through the head as he quavered in my Hav-a-Heart trap.

A cousin of mine used to eat one woodchuck a year. Because he lived by himself without an oven, he prevailed upon my grandmother to bake it. No one else in this house would touch the meat. Every Spring when I shot my first woodchuck in the Hav-a-Heart, I meditated eating him. I knew, after all, what filled his stomach and gave him leg muscle; I had ordered his victuals by seed from Burpee. Every Spring when the first chuck lay dead but unburied, I would look again at Irma S. Rombauer's woodchuck recipe in *Joy of Cooking*. Every year when I reread the part about wearing rubber gloves to skin the beast on account of the mites, I fetched the shovel from the toolshed and dug a hole deep enough so that dogs would not annoy the corpse.

I do not farm; less and less do I farm; physical work grows more and more alien. It isn't a general laziness; often I work a hundred-hour week. I keep a farmer's hours and a farmer's work week but avoid physical labor and raise no crops and milk no milk. I sit at my desk and put words on paper. When we first moved here to stay, I dreamed about replacing my grandparents. Mostly my dreams offered reasons and justifications: dreams for repairing trouble. My favorite was the morning when we woke (as I dreamed it) to discover that my grandfather and grandmother—very old but still living with us on the farm, still tending their hens, sheep, and cattle—were missing, nowhere to be found; what's more, the animals were gone. With the imperturbability that outfits some dreams, I decided that the old people must have dropped dead someplace while they were working; their bodies must be concealed by tall grass. We were about to give up the search and go back to our own work when we saw them coming toward us, still a couple of hundred yards away, walking up the narrow dirt road from Andover (the road was clearly dirt, road paved before I was born), waving and shouting to catch our attention: They were leading back to the barn a whole straggling line of ostriches, zebras, elephants, tigers, crocodiles. In my dream I understood that, because they were too old to continue farm-

ing, they had traded their Holsteins and merinos and Rhode
Island reds for zoo animals, for orangutans and lions, and I
knew as I woke that I felt poetry to be as exotic, beautiful,
scary, and useless as leopards and peacocks.

In May and June the green comes back.

Winter's white is beautiful when it begins but degenerates
by March to gray snow that melts mud-brown. Spring begins
as monochrome as November, but from the gray-brown, faint
green arises in grass that the sun heats. Then with more sunlight green mounts, gathers, swells, and explodes, its onrush-
ing upthrusting fibrous joy cavorting from the ground, yellow-
green to butter the soul's bread with. Down from the verdant
twigs of the trees, green descends toward green uprising, dog's-
ear leaves first unwrapping their tender delicate early edible
green, pale and lemony Spring-leaf green, later to darken or
weather into the green-shutter leaves of August.

Not until Spring's end does the bounty of Summer fore-
shadow itself in knuckled fingers of asparagus that hoist themselves through tall grass underneath the lilac. After a rain and
a hot day, asparagus leaps so rapidly that it goes by if we do
not harvest it daily. Every year we miss a dozen that go to
seed and grow tall as corn, wispy small trees in the breeze. The
first freshness of the year's crop, they are green heaven to the
mouth. And now peas bush and thicken, now rhubarb grows
green elephant ears over its strange ropey red-corded stalks.
Best of all, the old single roses by the driveway's bottom turn
green-leafed and bud a thousand tiny green buds that will welcome Summer, just after solstice every year, with pink flowers
and white. When they bloom they overpower the air with
sweetness, then shatter almost immediately. My grandmother
loved her old roses, and her small round gardens, marigolds
under the kitchen window and poppies at the edge of the hayfield by the barn. They rise green now making ready their
sweet violence.

Spring's greatest outburst happened earlier in the old days, and because it was the greatest I have saved it for last. In April between mud and blackflies, just before manuring and ploughing, my grandfather turned the cattle out to pasture. (Although it no longer happens on this farm, it never stops happening.) All Winter they stood upright in their stalls daylong, tied to wooden poles by steel chains. They lay down to sleep; they had plenty to eat; twice a day my grandfather unchained them to walk a few feet from tie-up to watering trough. They walked stiffly, down the one step and across frozen mud to the cement oblong trough to dip their pink noses into the just-unfrozen water. The surface froze every night and my grandfather lifted out big oblong pieces of ice. In January, in the shade and short daylight, Winter's icy litter left a series of trough-lids, like a sheaf of transparent pages. When the cattle drank their fill they stared around them, maybe dimly aware that they last saw this place twelve hours earlier, then each gave way to the next thirsty bossy and stiffly returned to the stalls where my grandfather left grain to encourage and reward their expeditious return.

One day in April their lives changed utterly. My grandfather kept an eye on the pasture grass, ready to spring his cattle loose. Snow and ice remained on the north side of sugar-maples and boulders, and in much of the pasture lowish sun penetrated only briefly and grass remained gray-brown, but where a clearing opened up in a high pasture, or where in lower patches new sun felt its way through a forest gap, live green grass rose edible in April. With crocuses came grass and with grass cow's paradise.

One day he untied them as if for the trough but maneuvered around them to open the pasture gate past the trough, portal to a hundred and thirty acres of Ragged Mountain: granite, hemlock, sugarbush, oak, elm, birch, and abundant grass. At first when he pushed and whooped them toward the gate they moved sluggishly. When they discovered themselves let out to pasture again, free to wander, free to eat all day long, their capacity for joy—these slow-moving mountains that usually made a name for lethargy and passivity, stoic mothers un-touched and unflappable—turned huge as their bodies: They jumped, they rubbed great sides against treetrunks, they leapt, they bellowed abruptly, they bounced. For a few moments the great Holsteins were eight kittens frolicking on the stomach of mothercat Ragged Mountain, play-fighting and romping. Then they let down their great heads into the sweet tender upgrowth of new grass and fed on the green milk of Spring as we all do, even in New Hampshire where Spring is the least of our seasons.

Summer

The longest day is the best day, when June twenty-second's pale light lasts into evening. In New Hampshire we are north enough to believe rumors from Scandinavia and Shakespeare about the madness of midsummer night's eve. Even contemporary England turns wild. I lived for a while in an East Anglian village where the morris men performed the Abbotts Bromley Horn Dance on midsummer night's eve. They waited until the ghostly late twilight of ten-thirty to wend down from the immense church on the hill—fifteenth century, with holy carving in stone and wood—through the graveyard already straggly with weeds, past the chestnut tree, almost as huge and old as the church, down Stony Lane past beetling medieval cottages that stonemasons working on the church inhabited for five generations. First danced the vicar playing a fife, followed by fiddlers in green, a dancing man suited up as a deer wearing green, two others carrying stag's horns, and at the rear two dancers with bows and arrows. Clearly the old religion survived at the solstice and the green man would be pierced by an arrow like William Rufus mistaken for an hind. We spent one year there in a 1485 house opposite the Guild

Hall and from our balcony watched the old troupe emerge from Stony Lane jigging to the eldritch tune. We sat with a poet friend visiting from England's north whose hair stood up as straight as grass. The next day as we walked between the church and the windmill a black cat streaked across our path and my friend leapt in the air; it was, he explained, the vicar.

The old religion stays underground in New Hampshire, or deep in the woods with Goodman Brown, but even here June twenty-second lofts gently out of this world. It begins early in the spirit-light of three-forty-five or so. When we are lucky the whippoorwill wakes us with his three syllables as brilliant as crystal, calling again, answering the call of a distant other, from the grass beside our bedroom window. The insistent triad continues for twenty minutes—*wake*-up-*now*, *wake*-up-*now* —and sets slugabeds cursing on every dirt road in New Hampshire. But if late sleepers erupt from their beds with mayhem on their minds, they are out of luck: The whippoorwill is elusive and we seldom catch glimpse of it. Brown, unpretty, it soars away to doze in its ground nest through sunlit hours.

Not only the whippoorwill wakes us on this long day and its briefer cousins of high Summer. Every bough bends with feathered guests singing of Summer in full-throated ease. Now the bluejay squawks and the fat crows caw—big as hens and black as evil where they gather on roadkills or on seeded fields —and the small birds trill, chirp, and exult or appear to exult; at least we exult as the pale light rises early casting a pink-yellow glow on the eastern slopes of Kearsarge. I walk outside blinking and stretching with the dog that blinks and stretches, performing The Dog from his yoga class, sniffing with total concentration. For him the nose and its pleasures and codes of knowledge are ten times more intense than my delighted vision. In the dog language there are two hundred words for squirrel piss.

Now I inhale cool morning air and feel cold wet dew on my toes in Summer sandals. The brief black tide of night withdrawn, the wet sand of morning emerges in vague light. An early squirrel tries the feeder that hangs from a branch on the great maple, squirrelproof squirrelsource, and gobbles his fill. Why not feed squirrels? I love these lithe tree-rats with bright eyes and nervous head-jerks that leap and run and fill mouths with grass for their nests and chase each other on the great trunks of old trees. Everywhere on lawn and hayfields we find round holes neatly cut into the ground, black Métro entrances for chipmunk, snake, mole, and vole. Gus the dog tries to give chase, which is why I leash him. Ada the cat spends all day on the breadbox watching birds; her life list fills a dozen pages. In the back garden where Jane tends flowers there is a stone retaining wall turned into cliff dwellings by chipmunks, skittery and quick, their furred cheeks bulging with tulip and crocus bulbs. Maybe the hummingbird is even more wonderful: In the hollyhocks, at the hosta, hummingbirds hover and flash. These overgrown bumblebees, biodegradable helicopters, athletes of stasis, fly or stand vibrating on air inches away from us all Summer long.

Summer is one continual morning under greeny leaves looking across greeny hayfields. When it diminishes it diminishes slowly, like our own aging and indistinguishable from it. When we claim that things aren't what they used to be we are always correct, though we may mistake diminishment's provenance. On the other hand, some things *do* get worse, even in the world outside: The whippoorwill is gone or going. My cousins who live on a dirt road away from our busy Route 4 still wake to hear him sing, but less often now. Four years ago we heard one whippoorwill, and since then none; ten years ago he was loud and many. Because he is shy, he is apt to avoid the highway, but traffic has not scared him away. He dies, he and his race; his old sapsucker generation narrows to disappear. How many years has DDT been prohibited? Yet DDT endures in the earth where we spread it once, and rises from the earth in blackfly livers that the whippoorwill eats. DDT thins whippoorwill eggshells so that they crack and the embryo dies that will not wake us in the morning to sing and to breed more whippoorwills. People sleep later in the morning.

•   •   •

Summer morning has its birdsong still and its clear pitchforks of energy. Then the day lengthens in silence and we work at our desks while the sun struggles past Ragged to rise in the sky. Because we are protected by Ragged and by outspreading elderly maples we don't take the sun's brunt until afternoon. The old house stays cool, even cold most mornings: a fire in the Glenwood. Usually once or twice in July and August I scrape thin ice from the windshield at five o'clock. On the hottest days, when the New Hampshire midday reaches the nineties, our house stays cool except for upstairs late in the afternoon. Occasionally it's humid but night cools down and by dawn it's cold; even during a hot patch we sleep breathing cool air.

Afternoons we go down to Eagle Pond; elsewhere it would be Eagle Lake, for this is not a circle of water with a few ducks in it; it's twenty-five acres, shaped like a humpbacked whale, shallow and muddy at its edge and deep in the center. Half a mile northwest is Eagle's Nest, a small camelhump hill where the bird lived that fed from the pond twice a day in my great-grandfather's time; Ben Keneston named our house Eagle Pond Farm when he moved here in 1865. He was thirty-nine years old, a sheepfarmer from Ragged with four children and more to come. My grandmother Kate, born at this place in 1878 when her father was fifty-two, never knew the eagle.

My great-grandfather owned the land around the pond. When my mother and her sisters went to Bates College and my grandparents needed cash for tuition, they sold land on the west side of the pond to provide space for a boys' camp; my mother remembers when they grew potatoes there. Over the years the camp expanded, buying land to the north that belonged to my Uncle Luther's son-in-law Jesse Johnson, and from my grandmother a large patch to the south end of the pond where we once pastured sheep, where they built a companion girls' camp and tennis courts. We still own the east side from the bridge by the beaver bog past a triangular field, then past a narrow steep slope where the railroad trench cuts near the pond, a few hundred yards north to a corner that be-

longed to Kate's older brother, my Uncle Luther, a Congrega-
tional minister who pastured his sheep beside the pond. Now
it's the Eagle Pond Motel.

Pond afternoons begin at the end of June, maybe the first
days of July, after the blackflies have largely departed. At the
little beach we cut into the east side of the pond tall hemlocks
and oaks screen the sun out until one or two in the afternoon.
We walk down a steep slope over slippery needles and weath-
ered oak leaves to our clearing on the mossy shore. A dozen
birches lean out over dark water. The water is dark with min-
erals; exiting the pond as it goes south under the bridge, it
turns into the Blackwater River. By the pond's edge under a
birch a tiny ancient rosebush blooms pink and brief at June's
turn into July. Ferns and oak saplings upthrust every Summer.
Moss sinks under our bare feet and sends up tiny red flowers.
We sit in canvas sling chairs beside the picnic table or lie in the
sun on Newberry's plastic chaises taking the breeze and the
warmth. These afternoons I stare a lot, imbecilic with pleasure,
at birches and ferns, at Eagle's Nest in the distance, and at
campers. The camp is remarkably unobnoxious. When I was
a boy it permitted me notions of superiority as I watched boys
of my own age marching to an indifferent drummer, or at least
hiking under the direction of a counselor. They didn't feed
chickens, load hay, or listen to old poems recited by a man
milking Holsteins in a tie-up. They played games, went on
hikes, practiced crafts, and sang songs; worst of all, they were
stuck with each other's company.

The camp is a comfortable affair where children from prosperous suburbs (on Parents' Weekend the camp road jams
with Mercedes) visit our countryside. A congregation of four
hundred children remains quiet, polite, and tidy: They don't
litter; they don't vandalize or make trouble. If we hear reveille
from an amplified tape in the morning and taps at night before
we go to sleep, these sweet sounds raise a frail frame against
our improvised day unstructured by clocks. The only un-
pleasant sound from the camp arrives during our pond after-

noons when the girls waterski; the motorboat growls and makes waves that erode our shoreline. Still, the one motorboat on Eagle Pond interrupts us for only an hour, as we observe the gaiety and terror of ten-year-old girls holding on for life. I tried feeling grumpy about it, but the pleasure of watching pleasure—all these skinny daughters—won me grudgingly over.

Otherwise, our afternoons at the pond are silent. I gaze at the landscape and at clouds; I look at a book; occasionally I write a line or a note toward a line but I don't call it working. Jane reads and soaks in sun. We swim a little, but mush and mussel shells underfoot, not to mention green corpsefinger weeds straggling in our faces, make swimming less than perfect. With Summer guests we laze talking and eat slow picnic suppers. Mid-August the campers leave. Jane turns melancholy as their departure plays taps for Summer, but there are compensations, like perfection of quietness. Great oaks rise moving uphill from the birches by the shore. These trees protect us and hide us. I like swimming out fifty yards so that I can turn around, float or tread water, and stare back at the place I mostly stare out from—at the succession or hierarchy of trees, from delicate ghost birches leaning so decoratively, to the brave hemlock, tall and straight like a tree destined to become the mast of His Majesty's frigate that will blockade the Spanish ports, to the great irregular oaks and the intermixture of smaller ash and popple. At the hilltop by the railroad rises a birch a yard thick.

Late August, early September, the last afternoons punctuate themselves with sounds of falling acorns. I make my annual acorn collection; I stare at them and try to understand why I love them so much. Often they come two together, tiny metallic smooth green breasts with sharp nipple points, knitted caps on top to end breasthood. I hold them, rub them, shine them; I take my favorites home to put on my desk where they turn brown and I throw them away.

Lying still we watch squirrels gathering acorns. Sometimes

if we keep quiet we spy a quick mink scooting under ferns and low bushes. We hear frogs chatter. If I walk back and forth along the water I cause a continual series of frog-splats by the startle my footsteps make; it is as if I were beating a drum. Now that the pond is depopulated we may see an enormous loon or jump at its terrifying cry. We have watched ducks all Summer, little platoons of ducklings hiding in coves from motorboats and campers, now growing larger. Canada geese fly over in huge flotillas, heading south.

Fish, flesh, and fowl commend all Summer long whatever is begotten, born, or dies. All Summer the creation thrives, wasps and roses. Tiny ants plague the kitchen. A bundle of wasps models a new nest under an attic eave. By the road at the end of June single old roses that budded late in Spring burst forth with petals pink and white for the briefest season, ancient flowers my grandmother loved as a girl a century ago, doubtless sniffed by early settlers born in the eighteenth century. Shy small frail petals outcurl only to fall, to litter the green earth with their iridescence, making another beauty for an hour. While they bloom we hover above them, taking deep and startling breaths, for their odor is all the perfumes of Arabia, ambergris of all whales of all Pacifics, wave upon wave of velvety sensuous sweetness. We bend, sniff, shake our heads, walk away, and return for more. We cut a few—as abundant as they're brief—to take to church or float in a bowl on the black Glenwood. Quick and fragile as the flowers are, the bushes are durable. All Winter snowploughs heap dirty drifts on them thick with salt. Sometimes the plough gouges their earth; we think they must have been damaged this year, but come the end of June they raise to the Summer air their proliferate odor.

Although the old farmers weren't known for their devotion

to beauty, they loved their flowers. While I hayed with my grandfather, working as hard as he did he would pause stockstill from time to time—maybe as we worked the Crumbine place and looked across the valley toward Vermont's hills—and sigh and praise the glory. My grandmother interrupted the million tasks of her household—making soap, pies, bread, doughnuts, jam, and jelly; canning, sewing, darning, knitting, crocheting, egg gathering, washing, ironing—to tend her flowers. She kept a small round garden in front of the kitchen window over the set-tubs where she spent so much of her life. I remember marigolds there, zinnias, pansies early, hollyhocks. Across the yard, past the far driveway at the lip of the hayfield, she tended a circle of poppies that dazzled their Chinese reds against the long wavy gray-green grass. Some Summers now a lone poppy rises in the field. In a tiny round bed by the road I remember my grandmother placing, among the green things, silvery burned-out radio tubes that she found beautiful. She loved a crockery birdbath that she ordered from Sears and set in front of the house and kept full of water where small birds routinely bathed. Also she stuck in the lawn painted wooden ducklings following a mother duck. In our back garden now we keep a wooden cutout of a girl in clogs watering a wooden cutout tulip. In front we favor whirligigs —a woodchopper, another milking a cow.

We say that the old farmers weren't known for their devotion to beauty, with their long work days and their residual Calvinism, but perhaps their inattention allowed them to cultivate beautiful things without self-consciousness. The shape of an old Cape is handsome—and the wooden-carved pillars at the corners of Greek temple farmhouses, and the elegant joints of barn beams, and the coherent stonework of walls. An old flower garden is not useful but as you walk in the dense woods of New Hampshire in Summer you know you are close to an old farmstead when you find the lilac and the old roses growing; the house is collapsed and even the cellarhole hardly distinguishable, but the farmwife's flowers endure.

Nor was it only in gardens and architecture that art showed itself. Theater groups in the villages put on annual performances. Yearlong, groups met once a fortnight to speak pieces, play the piano, and sing. We found in an old desk an 1890s record book containing the minutes of the South Danbury Oratorical and Debating Society, where my grandparents performed and courted. My grandmother played the piano; my grandfather spoke pieces, the same story-poems I heard in the tie-up fifty years later. After an hour in which citizens played, sang, and showed off for each other, they took coffee and then debated a topic like "Resolved: That the United States should undertake no further territorial expansion." Maybe they were more political than aesthetic—they were certainly more passionate about national politics than most of their descendants —but it is remarkable how much art and beauty entered their daily lives, whatever they called it. Shaker design is elegant, simple, clear, durable, classic; this austere sect never consciously sought beauty.

The Shakers who fascinated Hawthorne were numerous not so long ago. My mother remembers fainting once in Enfield when she was a girl; two Shaker ladies alighted from a carriage to help her. Although the women had difficulty climbing into and out of the wagon, and lifting my mother, the two Shaker men up front could not assist them because they could not touch them.

In front of the porch Jane grows tulips, poppies, Thermopsis, Campanula (carpatica, persicifolia, lactiflora), phlox, daffodils, crocus, Siberian iris, dwarf German iris, peonies, foxglove, coral bells, old-fashioned single hollyhocks, bleeding heart, astilbe—as well as lavender, lovage, thyme, and oregano. At the house's front on Route 4 she grows day lilies, ajuga, Shasta daisies, yarrow, watermelon poppies, and some poppies without names that Mary Jane Ogmundson gave her. In back she tends a secret garden paved with brick she laid; it is hidden enough from the road so that she can sunbathe. Here the old wellhead raises a platform that she covers with pots of basil, geraniums, strawberries with alyssum around the edge, fragrant Acidanthera, lobelia, nemesia, and browallia. There is a bench, a chair, and a pretty chaise; she has a cement swan-pot here, a cement lion, a terra cotta putto, a sundial, and a tall iron potholder spilling over with bleeding hearts. In the interstices of the bricks, Jane plants glory-of-the-snow. Around the base of the wellhead she grows buttercups.

Against the retaining wall that holds Ragged back she plants heather, peonies, Veronica (Crater Lake Blue), evening primrose, lamb's ears, artemesia (Silver Mound), dwarf asters, bee balm, Lysimachia clethroides, Jacob's ladder, more phlox, more Campanula, and more Siberian iris, red-twigged dogwood, and roses. On the hill above the wall, shading back to the ferns, oaks, and sugarmaples of Ragged Mountain, the Spring's daffs defer to wave after wave of day lilies, the regular orange kind so common we forget how beautiful they are, yellow trumpets from White Flower Farm called Hyperion and planted in memory of John Keats—day lilies plain and fancy. All Winter I sense Jane's silent presence in the dining room where she stands many-sweatered in the gloom, peering out into the back garden where bench and swan and sundial stick up through snow. She daydreams Summer, daydreams seeds and plants she will order and tend; her mind blooms with bright petals in gray February.

Where she grows her lilies my aunts in the 1930s made a rock garden. I remember masses of pinks. Neither Caroline nor Nan married young. Both schoolteachers, occasionally they traveled in summer, and Caroline took an M.A. at Yale Summer School, but mostly they returned to Eagle Pond Farm, to their father and mother and nephew. The sisters cleared a beach near our swimming place, which they called Sabine, and when I was little, before I started haying with my grandfather in 1941, I spent my afternoons paddling and swimming with them, collecting mussel shells and turtles, scaring frogs.

.   .   .

The greatest crop in New Hampshire's July and August, for
the last one hundred and forty years, is the Summer people.
I date them from the railroad but they came even earlier by
stagecoach and horseback. Mid-nineteenth-century prosperity
in the manufacturing North brought them before and after
the Civil War. The poets and essayists of New England came
to New Hampshire, and America's Alps sponsored a White
Mountain School of painting. Nathaniel Hawthorne, who
wrote many stories out of his New Hampshire trips—"The
Great Stone Face" about the Old Man, "The Ambitious Guest,"
"The Great Carbuncle," "The Canterbury Pilgrims" about a
Shaker settlement south of us—died in a hotel in Plymouth on
his way to the mountains for a holiday with his old Bowdoin
classmate the ex-president of the United States Frank Pierce.
Ralph Waldo Emerson had nasty things to say about citizens
of New Hampshire because he was annoyed with Daniel Web-
ster, the Massachusetts senator who was born here. Melville
and Thoreau came on foot and rowing a boat. William James
had a Summer place up north, and Henry visited him and
wrote beautifully in *The American Scene* about New Hampshire's Summer countryside. Henry Adams's great friend John
Hay—Lincoln's private secretary and biographer, later secretary of state under McKinley and the first Roosevelt—spent
every Summer on Lake Sunapee west of us.

They came by the thousands, women and children first, up
by trains from Boston away from the heat. Their husbands followed on weekends and for two weeks in August. At Potter
Place stages took them to New London, and to Elkins on Pleas-

ant Lake. My mother remembers when Harry K. Thaw, famous murderer of Stanford White over the girl in the red velvet swing, parked his private railroad car at Potter Place and with his keeper—Clarence Darrow copped an insanity plea for him; sprung from the insane asylum, he was required to keep a keeper—climbed Kearsarge and slept at the New London Inn. From West Andover's depot the stage took them to Springfield. Although there were lakes here and there, swimming was still an exotic pastime. People did not come north for water sports, nor for tennis or golf or anything except cool air. Huge old wooden inns rose on every hillside, some still standing, and the richest folks kept their own houses, or cottages as they called them. Halfway up Kearsarge, where the CCC made a parking lot and picnic area before the Second World War, stood Winslow House where the stage deposited Bostonians with trunks full of their clothes and even their china. Many visitors simply boarded at farms where they added plates to a table already large, occupied a spare room, and shared the outhouse.

Summer people were essential to the economy even before the collapse of farming. At the Pleasant Lake Inn—handsome with all its gables at the west end, with a splendid view of Kearsarge rising beyond the water—my Great-Aunt Nanny cooked all Summer. Families spent Summers at the same address for a hundred years. Children from Massachusetts and New Jersey grew up identifying July and August with Lake Sunapee, with Springfield or Danbury or Enfield.

These months make islands of guiltless hours away from school and the rules of Winter; the Summer place becomes a mental state, a name for sweet freedom, innocent irresponsibility, imagination's respite, time for loafing and inviting the soul. Poets of place hymn paradisal castles of Summer: Poets as diverse as Charles Olson and T. S. Eliot write eloquently of their different Gloucesters. Now in our backwoods of New Hampshire, many permanent citizens are emigrants or descendants of emigrants from city and suburb, and a small but valuable contingent are children of the Summer vacationers who came to love the landscape not only as interchangeable scenery—cards in a deck that flip through Switzerland, Mexico, Ireland, Peru, and Hilton Head—but as the heart's green and granite, and who, exposed to the rural culture, chose to join it.

On the other hand, many Summer visitors care nothing for place or people—and people return the gesture. Every June we complain, at first of traffic and then of bad manners, discourteous behavior in the aisles of the supermarket, condescension, and arrogance. We have become The Natives, amusing rustics perhaps, more likely vendors suspected of exploitation. Year-rounders turn grumpy. Of course it is a perennial conflict wherever tourists congregate, as ineluctable as town-and-gown in the neighborhood of a college. When I feel scorn for July's hordes I try to remember that I started that way. Or almost. I grew up living the school year out in suburban Connecticut, Ardmore Street in Hamden—four miles from the center of New Haven, two miles from the Brock-Hall Dairy Company, which my grandfather co-founded and where my father worked. When I came north for Summers I was not exactly a vacationer: I didn't go to a hotel or a rented cottage or a lakeside camp; I went to the house where my mother and my grandmother were born and grew up; I worked in the hay-fields; briefly I joined the back-country culture that was so alien to Spring Glen Grammar School and the values of the blocks. I inhabited for a while the universe of church suppers, Christian Endeavor, outhouses, cowmanure, chickens, Civil War stories, whitewash in the tie-up, cellarholes, fishing, poverty, straw-chewing, and Rawleigh's Salve.

It was not only a farm in the country I went to; it was an entire dying world. When I took the New York, New Haven, and Hartford to Boston, from South Station to North, I crossed a line almost century-wide. The train I climbed onto in North Station was a time machine and the conductor a hundred years old; he wore a handkerchief between his collar and his neck for the sweat. The benches were hard in the old cars, and the

Boston and Maine train, after leaving suburban Boston and southern New Hampshire, stopped every two miles. This was the Peanut, last passenger train of the afternoon, originally the next-to-last because its name derived from *pénult*. While we chugged north layers of Hamden peeled away from me as if I shed a skin: Concord, Penacook, Boscawen, Franklin, East Andover (called Halcyon), Andover, West Andover (called Gale)—and the old handkerchiefed conductor set the yellow step on cinders and I alighted to find my grandfather grinning as he whispered comforting words into the ear of a bony horse harnessed into the arms of an ancient carriage. Soon the train puffed away on its journey north—three miles to South Danbury (called Converse) just past the church—and with my suitcase lodged in back of the seat, behind Riley we started the mile journey home. My world was transformed: no car, no tractor, no school, no classmates. The whole Summer I joined the historical past, entered it as if through a door, took part in it, played the part, lost myself in it and in love of it.

My old world I preferred to my new. From the moment of the depot until the moment ten weeks later when I reversed the slow melancholy journey, taking the morning Peanut for Boston, I joined the country of the grandparents—I have written this before; before I die I will write it again—and I loved it a thousand times more. Here was diversity: old and young, sick and healthy, rich and poor, all together. One definition of the suburbs is segregation: The greens live on one block and the blues on another. Here was eccentricity, affection, humor, freedom, and stories. Here of course were grandparents, not parents; this place had not been freedom for my mother. This place was not innocent irresponsibility or imagination's respite for the farmer who grappled yearlong in its sandy soil.

All Summer I worked but I did not work hard. The chicks were my domain, and I brought them water and grain at morning and at night. Afternoons were haying. I stood atop the old rack with its split pole rails while my grandfather pitched hay up and I tucked it in place and trod to weave it together. On the way to the hayfield and on the way back my grandfather talked, told stories, and recited poems. This was the best part, but even the work was good. I keep bright intact recollections of these afternoons: On a hot day I stand in the breeze on top of the hayrack looking down on valley and pond; I am thirteen and my grandfather will never die.

Because I did not belong to the country the whole year, the whole life, I was a Summer person. A suburban child, I preferred the rural, archaic, old, and eccentric. I took my mother's New Hampshire over my father's Connecticut. I chose it and I choose it. When I was eleven or twelve I daydreamed living here year round, a lonely trapper on the hill like all the bachelor solitaries who lived cramped into tumbledown shacks. By the time I was sixteen I daydreamed of living here as a writer; in my twenties I learned that this was impractical; in my forties I did it. Now if I grumble about Summer people, doubtless I protest in order to separate myself from what I was or partly was. It is easy to make stereotypes, harder to make distinctions. Many long-term Summer people feel connected to landscape and to people by way of rural culture; their Summers are not only climate, pond, and hill but islands of country ethic and culture, which they cherish against the life they lead at other times. They return to old cottages they renew each year, and they pay taxes and keep up their own land. Although in the stereotype Summer people are rich, in truth many are not. I think of Clarence and Katherine Grimes who came to Stinson Lake for fifty years. Clarence taught German and French and music at Hamden High School in Connecticut where I spent two years; Katherine was a painter and a cellist. On a high school teacher's salary they bought land in the thirties and built a camp and brought their children every year and later their grandchildren, and when Kay died in 1985 Clarence buried her in a tiny graveyard over their camp where he stays Summers still, lonely in his ninth decade.

On the other hand, a new breed buys condos and cuts off

our view of the blue mountain. They purchase air and sun
for their pleasure, as if the creation were not common inheri-
tance, glory, and obligation. Greed is not only theirs but also
the farmer's who sells his land and the developer's who sub-
divides it—but it is also theirs who grant the farmer and the
developer their money; their greed is for exclusiveness. On
the west side of Newfound Lake there's a patch of road where
I used to drive, looking across choppy blue water at firs and
hills on the other side, but now saw-tooth brown-shingle condos, between road and water, remove Newfound Lake from
public vision. They bought the view; for the first time in mil-
lennia, since the glacier set it there, the lake and the land are
split apart.

John Morse hays our fields at June's end, cutting, turning hay
that gets rained on, raking and baling it with a series of ma-
chines hooked up to his tractor: very like a horse. When he and
his strong boys gather the bales onto a pick-up truck, they
work a long day shirtless in the bright sun and in the early
evening stand resting in the long shadows. (In the Fall after
slaughter John returns our grass transformed into lamb roast
and steak.) The stubble hayfield looks brown for a week or
so; then it softens into green again, rises, and waves when the
wind blows. Where the long grass ripples my grandfather
grew tall fieldcorn; every Summer when I was small I lost myself in it on purpose, in order to be frightened and enjoy the
comfort of salvation.

For twenty-five years after my grandfather died hay remained abundant, growing from topsoil composed of a century
and a half of Holstein manure. But underneath lies sand the
glacier left. One year not long ago John stacked half as many
bales as he had the year before, and we knew the goodness had
leached out of the soil. Now John limes the fields in Autumn;
we talk of ploughing, harrowing, replanting with new seed,
and fertilizing. Whatever we do, we want to keep the fields.
A hayfield grown up to bushes is melancholy. These Sum-

mers I drive past dense groves of trees where I spent afternoons
in the 1940s haying with my grandfather. Trees are beautiful
and wood is useful but cleared land is a monument to the old
settlers. Think of the labor that cleared it: cutting, stumping,
burning the timber it didn't pay to haul; oxen sledding great
stumps and granite boulders. How different the land looked a
hundred years ago. On the slopes of Ragged, even of Kearsarge, stonewalls border deep forest. Stonewalls weren't built
to keep pine trees in; somebody cleared it for pasture and kept
it clear. Up on highway 89 as you approach Hanover, great
domed hills rise, clear with pasture and hayfield. The hills of
our Ragged, and much of New Hampshire, domed clear and
green under the yellow light of Summer a century ago.

Summer is a series of special events. On the Fourth of July,
little flags from Memorial Day still wave over the graves of the
veterans, but Independence Day is less patriotic than it used
to be. Maybe I remember it from an especially military time,
1942–45, but now it seems to be a child's day or a day to be
childish on. Andover specializes in the glorious Fourth. There
are crafts for sale, hot dogs and balloons, and at eleven we
watch the long parade of floats, horses, bands, antique cars,
and fire engines—the same ones that parade for Danbury at
the Grange's Harvest Festival in September, that spend the
year traipsing from parade to parade. Andover's own Lions
club parades a Concord coach hauled by a brace of horses,
Leslie Ford as coachman, that galavants all over the state—
at Danbury, at Warner's Fall Festival, at the Lions' soccer
match between Vermont and New Hampshire. On the morning of the Fourth the Lions do a breakfast at Andover School
—pancakes and sausage, real syrup—as they do on a Saturday
in deer season. Lunch is everybody's chuck wagon. Supper is
sometimes a church, sometimes the Volunteer Fire Department back at the school about the time the midway opens:
turtle races, a tethered balloon, try your strength, throw soggy
baseballs at wooden milk bottles. When supper's cleared the

bingo starts, also staged by the Lions, and when it is dark come the fireworks: sudden night-flowers, orange and red and green and gold and silver, erupting against the black of night.

Summer is also the South Danbury Church Fair, later in July. The committee that plans the fair meets a few weeks ahead. First we decide who's on the Supper Committee, because that's the biggest job, five or six women who will cook for a week, then dish it out, keep it flowing, and clean up afterward—three and a half frantic hours. The Supper Committee needs outside help. Every Summer several of the hardest working women are not churchgoers; they support the church that will bury them, working like crazy once a year, but they draw the line at sitting in a pew on a Sunday.

Our White Elephant Committee sells odds and ends; our Food Committee sells bread, brownies, and doughnuts. Another committee collects handicrafts and fancy work; we have a committee for grabs and another for tonic. Two or three husbands do set-ups the night before the fair, gathering picnic tables from all over town. On the fair Saturday, our tables open at four, followed by supper at five. People get in line by four-forty-five, and dishing up usually starts early; everything is early by New Hampshire time. (If friends are due at our house for a meeting at seven, we know to be ready for early arrivals at six-thirty.) During supper and after there will be homemade ice cream, always prepared and sold by Joe and Marilyn Bouley and Audrey Curren. Final event of the day is our annual auction. I'm on the Auction Committee, a male estate.

To cook for supper, I cross the line, contradicting a cultural gender-value, coming out of the closet with cooking. But I display no reticence: I walk up and down the supper line, urging, "Don't miss the turkey salad. Try the meatloaf." My cousin Ansel who is a great baker has always cooked quantities of magnificent rolls but they pass for Edna's. Mary Smith cooks prodigious amounts of everything. Doris Huntoon does also. Pies and casseroles and salads come from Bertha, Vicki, Jane Powers, Martha, Audrey, Dorothy, Ruth Houghton, Ruth

True, Phyllis, Marion, Mary Lyn, Joan and Lois, Annie, Vera, Kendra, and Trudy. Along with pies and casseroles, Dot Heath makes funky beans, and equally funky, wholly different beans arrive from other kitchens. Jane cooks a thousand loaves of French bread for the food table; she makes more rolls and three casseroles and salads of macaroni, fruit, and mixed vegetables. We have dozens of pies and cakes; Edna's red velvet cake annually shakes our heads with its startling deep crimson.

We dish supper outdoors in front of the church and eat at tables set around it. Every year we feed more than a hundred people for $3.50 apiece and less for children, cheap even for New Hampshire. Recently I heard of volunteer firemen charging $6 for a chicken barbeque supper. It must have been over by Center Sandwich. Last Summer my wife read her poems there, a town of elegant, precise old Capes not far from Squam ("Golden Pond") and Winnipesaukee. In the audience every head was a distinguished gray, and the white ducks came from Brooks Brothers. Somebody said in the question period, "There's a lot of people in New Hampshire, but you never meet anyone who was born here." It astonished me to hear the line, spoken so often about California or Arizona, Colorado or Florida, applied to my state; and I shuddered to recognize the portent. In the Danbury crowd at our fair, most were born here; the bronze tablet at the Town Hall, where Danbury lists boys who fought in the Civil War, could almost be used for a list of voters. But in Wilmot or Andover, above all in New London, there are not so many natives; someday the South Danbury Church Fair will become an exercise in nostalgia.

Last Summer it rained. We had to move the fair three miles north to the Grange Hall in Danbury Village. Sale tables occupied the auditorium upstairs; we ate supper downstairs at tables fixed in place next to the Grange's kitchen, handy except that it lacks water. I sat by the top of the stairs selling tickets for supper, which this year meant that I had to be a negative maitre d', holding the line upstairs when there were no more seats in the dining room.

When supper's over, and the exhausted kitchen crew finally

eats what's left—beans, a corner of macaroni and cheese, some rolls, peach pie, carbs and more carbs—we hold our annual auction. Sometimes I auctioneer a little, but I am no good at it. This year, on the Grange's main floor, in front of the curtain with Kearsarge painted on it (normally we hold the auction in the little hillside amphitheater next to the church, where stables used to shelter horses and carriages from snow), my cousin Forrest filled in capably for Bill McKenzie who had to be away. Strong and burly with a great mustache, Forrest is a comic: If there's a blouse to auction he will model it. We sell junk mostly—a lawnmower without the shaft, a wagon seat without the wagon, a dish strainer, boxes of Reader's Digest Condensed Books, radios and record players and toasters (handymen's specials) and a mixmaster with one beater missing. Three years ago we enjoyed a brief harvest of beds, bunkbeds, tables, and chairs—big-ticket items—and we took in the dough. I act as change-maker, trudging up and down the little hill delivering goods; that was the year somebody with New York plates gave me a hundred dollar bill to change. (I had to crack the supper till.) Most years we make more laughter than money, as Bertha and Peter who are brother and sister bid against each other, as Pat challenges Ansel. Pat runs a perpetual yard sale and acquires stock every year from our auction. Toward the end, great boxes lump leftover items from the white elephant and the craft tables. One carton may gather a used whiskbroom, two pairs of ancient shoes, an issue of *Yankee*, sheet music from 1954, a three-way plug, two ashtrays, a package of pink sponges, a pale green crocheted pillow six inches by eight, a Snoopy washcloth, a cat's flea collar, part of an alarm clock, a broken cheeseboard, and three dozen plastic forks. This box goes for 25 cents, generally to Marge.

Mid-August is Old Home Day, Danbury one Sunday and Wilmot the next. Each town alternates the location among its tiny centers: Wilmot Flat, Wilmot Center, or North Wilmot; Danbury Village or South Danbury. Wherever it happens it repeats certain rituals; wherever it happens it is a diminished thing. The governor proclaimed Old Home in 1899 because of New Hampshire's depopulation. For decades people had left the farms for the mills where the hours were shorter and the pay steady; then the farms became increasingly poorer because on better and flatter land to the west farmers could use more machinery and fewer hands.

My mother, born in 1903, remembers hordes arriving for Old Home when she was a girl. Wilmot's took place at the Methodist Camp Ground where cottages sprouted among tall pines like the mushrooms of a wet Summer; the 1938 hurricane smashed pines onto the tiny cottages and ended the Camp Ground. (We still travel Camp Ground Road.) Even I can remember two hundred gathering there in the midthirties: My grandfather bought me vanilla cones, my Uncle Luther the minister addressed the multitude, and on the bandstand the old men of Moulton's Band from Sanbornton, in blue caps and uniforms with red piping and epaulets, played marching songs and hymns that marched. In my mother's day, maybe until the Second War, local residents staged a play for the exiles' reunion, and a dance my mother couldn't go to. Rumor had it some of the fellows drank hard cider.

Stagecoaches and primitive buses waited at the depot for the diaspora's return. There were prizes for those who came from the greatest distance—Pennsylvania, Tennessee, Ohio, even Idaho; for the largest family groups, from great-grandparents to infants, thirty-seven at a whack; for the eldest attending, usually late nineties or a hundred, possessor as eldest citizen of the *Boston Post* cane that persisted as badge of superior antiquity long after the *Post* died (my grandmother was proud of being eldest several years running); and for the youngest, always a babe in arms.

We still give the prizes but we are a remnant repeating a ritual after its purpose is mostly gone. Only forty of us gather. Although the eldest is still usually a nonagenarian, the youngest is sometimes four or five; the farthest journeying comes from Boston; the largest family may be six. The original emigrants are dead, and their children's children lived in seven cities before they were ten years old, none of them in New Hampshire. Still, Old Home Day remains another pleasant and innocent excuse for gathering. Always a few old friends and former residents schedule an annual visit to coincide with Old Home. My mother who lives in Connecticut has not missed many. After the morning sermon we eat a picnic lunch and listen to the current Moulton's Band from Sanbornton playing Beatles songs adapted for brass—and John Philip Sousa also. After the band concert we move inside for a program. We sing songs like "Old New Hampshire" and "New Hampshire People," which goes to the tune of "Auld Lang Syne." We sing one called "Wilmot's Sons and Daughters," which Stella Collins wrote long ago:

> To the joyous din of welcome,
> Wilmot joins with hearty voice
> As her fast returning children
> Make the old heart to rejoice.
>
> While Kearsarge still towers above us,
> Strong and steadfast, calm and grand,
> To her absent sons and daughters
> Wilmot holds a beckoning hand.

Usually there's a talk. Two years ago Walter Walker showed slides he'd taken at old Old Homes, a popular program. We sat in the Town Hall with shades drawn on a warm dry afternoon late in August looking at our dead in Ektachrome. Often on the weekend of Wilmot's Old Home the camps close down across the pond. Long lines of chartered Vermont Transit buses raise dust on Eagle Pond Road, and young campers crowd at the windows saying farewell for another year to Eagle Pond and Ragged Mountain.

We get to stay. We linger at pondside for a few more weeks of warm water in perfect stillness. Then one night, warned by the *Concord Monitor*, we cover tomatoes with poly, and in the cold morning I scrape ice from the windshield. Two or three icy mornings turn the pond chilly; along the shore we spy the first gay fires of Fall.

Fall

Waking in late September, we gaze south toward Kearsarge from the dawn window under the great maple that torches the hillside. Each morning is more outrageous than the one before, days outdoing their predecessors as sons outdo their fathers. We walk out over the chill dew to audit glorious wreckage from the night's cold passage —new branches suddenly turned, others gone deeper into ranges of fire, trees vying to surpass each other and their yesterselves. In the afternoon we take long walks with Gus, who is the color of oakleaves, who bounds ahead of us and leaps to chase a leaf falling. Maybe we take New Canada, the dirt road that climbs the northwest slope of Ragged Mountain, and promenade in a tunnel of red shade under oak and maple, under wide old birches with leaves a delicate yellow. On the downslope, as leaves fall away the valley opens, and for the first time since April we can look across toward hills of Vermont visible on the clearest day. As the dog bounces our hearts bounce also with a happy overload, our landscape turned into sensuous Italian crockery or grand opera staged by the cold hills.

Or we walk on the low dirt road that skirts Eagle Pond, and on the rattling bridge at the south end—over the Blackwater River's tributaries exiting the pond, by the beaver's bog where wet earth stabs upward with gnawed stumps of popple—we stand and stare with our jaws gaped at the tweedy circumference of the pond, low trees turned orange, Chinese red, pink, russet, together with silver-gray trunk and evergreen green, weaving the universe's most outlandish fabric, the whole more purple than not, although no part of it is purple.

Walking back to our house from any direction, we know again and always for the heart-stopping first time that our house sits floating in the center of Autumn's flood: yellow-candle leaves against unpainted barn; wild fiery maple up-shooting against the sprawling old white house with green shutters; the slope of Ragged rising behind with its crazy anthology of universal color, shade, and texture. We inhabit the landscape's brightest and briefest flesh.

Or we drive, dangerous as it is—who can watch the road?—to places we remember. Driving on I-89, up where the Connecticut River Valley opens, we ride high discovering enormous vistas of Fall's bounty, the distant low hills giving off their variegated light. But middle distance is best. Close up we see the one leaf and the one tree, gorgeous but myopic; long distance makes a momentary uniformity; best middle distance offers tricks of focus, and as we drive by certain mild hills— mild the rest of the year—we take them in as leaf, as tree, and as expressionist wild canvas. The eye learns a rapid oscillation that makes all-parts and one-whole into yet another whole: creation's apotheosis and heaven on earth. Past Danbury east on 104 there's a moment of space, north of Ragged where the ski folks go in Winter, where the land widens into a sudden plain, flat as water and the size of Eagle Pond. Here we park in October to stare. Over the brief plain the hills start again, bright in the middle distance.

Or driving back from Franklin, where we shop at the A & P or go to Keegan's Hardware, or from Tilton where Bob Beaulieu sells the best cheese and corns his own beef, we take the back road from East Andover to Andover Village. This narrow road rides straight up and down, past abandoned farms and great farmhouses, some with their elms surviving, one Victorian and huge where Governor Batchelder lived, some with stony pastures cleared two hundred years ago and not yet grown over. At the edge of this road stands a magnificent Federal house with a fanlight over the door, square and upright white clapboard, with a little family graveyard, with a view of noble Kearsarge and with Ragged's southern slope in the grandeur of middle distance.

Then leaves fall. They turn, they alter, and they fall. The trees that turn first drop leaves first, swampmaples shedding into their damp boggy earth, upsticking their twigs as the slower trees on the hills behind them start their journey. Then birch, popple, ash, and the great maple inaugurate their denuding, at first in the chill vinegary air one and two leaves spiraling; then by the dozen the colorful leaves diving and dancing down, divers and dancers staggering through air to rest on silvery grass; then by the hundreds the leaves reeling down, making the air solid with swirling leaf-confetti, sketching the wind's whirling shapes on a cool morning. Oh, to stand in the woods or by the house, with the chill wind in our hair, surrounded and gently touched by the continual descent of the multitudinous reds and yellows of the abundant and generous trees. Only the oaks hold on, cherishing still their crimped brown leaves through Winter and even into Spring.

Rain is the enemy of brilliance. Some Autumns when the reds and yellows blaze their fiercest, three days of cold rain drain color out. Rain knocks the bright leaves down and removes their stain, so that if you kick at a leaf on the brown earth of the driveway, you find underneath it, like the imprint left by a child's cellophane transfer, the leaf's bright image intact and quick on the dirt. These years the pomp is brief, abrupt, and poignant. But Autumn is always poignant.

Fall, I would rather call it, as in dying fall or the fall of man. I think it was September when Adam and Eve left the garden, struggling as they walked on rough footing, the first time anyone did, uphill into the compromised world. Outside Eden the live pulsing green, thick flesh of leaf and stem, showed red wounds for the first time, withered beige and gray stalk, the bruised russet and yellow of dying vegetation. Against the uniform green of continual Summer advanced the complexities of Autumn, Fall's multivalent messages of decay in color and shape, death's mothering sigh. A leaf falls, the year falls, men and women fall. And, *felix culpa*, Fall is the most beautiful season—at least in New Hampshire.

Some of us spend our lives preferring Fall to all the seasons, accepting Winter's blank as the completion or fulfillment that our season presages, taking Spring only as prologue, and Summer as the gently inclined platform leading all too slowly to the annual dazzle. We are in love—not half-in-love, and not with easeful death—with the vigor of decay, as if we were philanderers bored by any gorgeous nineteen-year-old, all smooth skin and taut roundedness; merely tolerant of the *femmes de trente ans* whose bodies, softer and more serious, bloom with the secret growth of the sensual life; pursuing not young girl nor bloomed beauty but the gray-haired, stark-cheekboned beautiful woman of fifty.

For amorists of October, the red branch is the sign we seek. If we find it in May or June it only mocks us, for it is not earned and appropriate aging but disease, acid, blight, salt, herbicide, or a plague of beetles—mocking the splendor of Autumn as progeria, wretched aging-disease of children, mocks residents of the nursing home. But in August we may reasonably look for a touch of the true and natural red that flames at a maple branch's tip; even in August, with vagaries of elevation, temperature, storm, and moon, a minifrost foreshadows splendor. Though noon be hot, though well dry up and hay turn brown, though we parch tossing bales and rush to the lake for cool, yet the air is cold every morning. We rise to light a fire in the Glenwood, taking the chill off and the damp of cold dew, and to glance outside through early mist: *Is there more red on the hill?*

Every August somebody's garden goes. By Eagle Pond we are protected from early frost by the water's heat. But north of us toward Danbury, and west at Wilmot Flat, we watch for August's Autumn. When somebody loses her garden, we hear when we drop into the post office or the store: "Buck's folks got frosted out this morning." Driving past the Buck place, we see tall corn browning and withered, tomato plants blackening heavy with green-yellow globes. It is melancholy and no joke. From the peas planted early, scattered on snow in April; through the rototilled wet soil of May; through planting while blackflies assault the planter; through radishes, peas, frail carrot tops emerging, and beets; through struggles with woodchucks and deer onward to the battle with coons over corn; through weeding in July's heat and watering in the drought of early August—gardens are hard duty. A frost in late August or early September is enough to drive a family to drink or Arizona.

Safe with our garden, we look for the red branch. As September starts, we rise to white patches on grass that keeps its dark green. We glance at the tomato plants by the porch: They appear untouched; near the house and its reflected heat, sometimes they last into October.

Today it will warm up, and even turn hot for an hour early in the afternoon, but with a clear sky, tonight will be cold again. The million stars, so bright and harsh they prick at eyeballs, will see another frost. Somewhere somebody's tomatoes will blacken and sag. This morning, taking lunch at Blackwater Bill's, I hear one old man, entering, ask another old man at the counter, "How did your garden fare?"

From the red branch on the green tree, Fall enlarges to become the red tree on the green slope, where one maple of a hundred chooses to charge first into the breach. Then in September, in the damp places where swampmaples flourish, gross splendor begins: Swampmaple leads the way, groves of the small bushes or trees, in Spring and Summer scarcely worth our attention as they plume their frail green in marshy land beside meadows, unremarkable in a landscape of great oaks, of elms rare now even in New Hampshire, and of true maples in the dark sugarbush. In September these weed-trees take their brief hour on the stage. Swampmaples are the pioneers of Autumn, Daniel Boones or even Columbuses of the new world to come. They blaze with their Chinese reds, brilliant enamels sudden on a cool morning. While their noble cousins-by-name, rock maple of the hill, together with skinny poplar and pale birch, keep intact their dark almost black Summer green, green-shutter dark, swampmaples explode like Fourth of July nightworks, small red-fire fountains on low land. Driving to the P.O., I watch for the boggy patch a mile this side of Danbury where swampmaples congregate; here, on a sharp morning, a crimson eloquence rises like Godzilla from the bog.

The oldest metaphor makes Autumn a painter, Jack Frost with his manic palette. In the verdant context of August, when the first branch bursts red on the green tree, this quick eruption draws the eye as the hosta sucks the hummingbird in, and the hollyhock the honeybee. It is seductive enough, but it is subtle compared to the wild cacophony of late September and early October which blares and magnifies itself, synaesthetician mixing glaciers and violins, car horns and kangaroos, cowflops and electronic spacemusic. Deep Autumn is a *beautiful* Godzilla, wildest of wild beasts. Abrupt shreds and edges of New Hampshire turn fauve, while most of the northern hemisphere remains vague, impressionist, and *pretty*. Here we become Van Gogh for the yellow of sunflowers, Gauguin for the skin of oak leaves rich and sensuous, Hans Hofmann for the loaded, overloaded, dripping explosions or onslaughts of RED.

In Summer when cattle eat rich grass heavy with seed their udders fill so tight that they drip milk while they wait their turn for milking; the colorist's Autumn palette drips milk never white but red, sunflower yellow, green as pine or hem-

lock. Here in northern New England nothing is restrained—
in a culture where restraint is rumored to be the tint of the
soul. No, it's wild opera, all finale from overture on, and every
leaf ranges through octaves from soprano to bass, Yma Sumac
indeed, Yma Ash, Yma Birchtree, and above all Yma Maple—
composer and company collaborating on arias brilliant with
contrast, gross gorgeous vulgar screeches of color, unlimited
banquets of edible sense. If it were a cuisine, New Hampshire
Fall would combine curry powder, maplesyrup, garlic, tutti-
frutti, basil, scallions, chocolate black as the human heart,
chile relleno, fresh pineapple, and Coleman's mustard—
chopped and hashed together, mayhap, in the Cuisinart of
the middle distance.

We are all art critics of the annual exhibition, and we are
always mildly disappointed. "Why, sure," we say, "it's just
fine . . . but it's not bright like it was *last* year." In the actual
year, leaves never burn with a fire so wild as the conflagrations
of the arch-year in the mind's gallery.

Of New Hampshire I speak, not of the Midwest, which is
colorful but subdued, nor of the duochrome West Coast: California is green-if-it-rains, Arizona is brown-since-it-doesn't.
Michigan's Fall is like Europe's: burnished old gold; yellow
harvest mellow with violins; Autumn of the falling fruit and
the long journey toward oblivion; muted and melancholy; that
time of year where yellow leaves or none or few do hang;
where looking on the happy Autumn fields, we fall to thinking of the days that are no more. Autumn is English Johnny's,
season of mists and mellow fruitfulness, gorgeous and monochrome. Or if Autumn be French, let the long sobs of its violins pierce our hearts with languor and, indeed, monotony.
Europe never reaches the cacophony of New Hampshire's October with its purple cymbals and vermilion kettle drums, with
driving red trumpets and Edgard Varèse carcrash-codas of metallic jumble and roar. European Autumn is a dust of centuries
over the painter's light, brown cracked varnish aging, taking
Winter's oncoming darkness into itself.

In New Hampshire, October's detonation is flesh, opera, and expressionist cooking, but one must admit that it lacks structure. Like everything that we love this effect changes and turns into its opposite. By mid-November the cuisine alters to New England Boiled Dinner, wherein four hours of boiling blends corned beef and cabbage and onion and potato and turnip into the one salty tang. If Jack Frost starts expressionist he ends constructivist. Braque the brief fauve takes a six-week journey to Braque the analytic cubist. Crazy gorgeous canvas turns wire sculpture, and Willem de Kooning becomes Naum Gabo.

By Autumn's end all colors leave—or *almost* leave. To November's connoisseur the grades of beiges and grays, adjusting their textures, assemble colors as dear in their faintness as any orange whoops of September. Form, shape, and line take over, as egregious tweed hillsides shed orange, red, purple, and saffron. Darkening shreds of old leaves hang on the oaks, russet descending to earth-color, red-squirrel fur; then the gray-squirrel treetrunk advances with its frost-silver, vertical scored with vertical lines, against which rise vertical birches swooped and tilting (Ice-storms do that) with horizontal Mondrian-lines to contradict the white pillar of the trunk. And everywhere the rich dark evergreen. We assemble together, on the November canvas: green triangles, persisting serious heaving greens of hemlock, fir, and pine; vertical grays and vertical whites; slim horizontals of twig and birch-score; crumpled russet-gray of oakleaf and puffball. Now dead weeds straggle, gray stonewalls outline irregular rectangles, and emerging granite boulders push like whales with their great shoulders through the gray-brown sea of fallen leaves. Finally we reach the shape of the durable enduring world, fundament, skull underneath the flesh of shouts and colors. We arrive at line and form, without feeling except feeling for line and form, strong in what they omit and what they oppose: Son and daughter attack nothing so much as the loins they start from. Fall that begins as a Latin Quarter of passionate disorderly violent color—not so much French as Spanish, not so much

Spanish as Italian, and not Italian of Pope and Doge, of Cara-
vaggio and Michelangelo, but Italian of Cellini's breasted
saltcellar and equally breasted self-esteem, or Italian of twen-
tieth-century graveyard and wedding party—this Fall dis-
solves flesh or flesh falls away to reveal that in proper Heracli-
tean fashion the bones under the flesh are flesh's opposite.

Order and taste turn Japanese, the garden that is the analytic
palette a thousand years early: beige sand and gravel, raked
for direction without motion, sand-sea or frozen desert against
the arranged precise madness of miniature mountains, arti-
ficial Fujis of restrained romantic grays and gray-blues; mean-
while, on every side the framing gray-green moss, Kyoto's
evergreen, and rocks that make more borders. New Hampshire's November is Zen cubist de Stijl.

Earlier, Labor Day is a holiday truly celebrated hereabouts,
for it is the day when THEY go home, the Summer people who
arrive blooming late in the month of June. Everywhere gross
Oldsmobile stationwagons back up to cottages, loading leftover
Stolichnaya, unread stacks of Summer unreading, Port Salut,
golfclubs, tennisrackets, dental floss, and bottles of tanning
lotion. At hundreds of lakesides Volvos lift wing-hatches; at
mountain cottages fleets of Mercedes load themselves with
Summer's surplus commodity fetishism. Then down the long
I-ways—91, 89, 95—expensive cars crammed with tanned flesh
creep toward the suburbs of Boston and New York, even unto
New Jersey. THEY stretch and unload late at night in the blocks
of neighborhoods among prosperous twelve-room houses and
three-car garages . . .

While up north, in the countryside, air thins, lightens,
chills, and cheers up. No more traffic jams down to the post
office! No more bumping and shoving in the aisles at Cricen-
ti's! Browning hayfields, mountain, dirt road, and stonewall
return to us. The land is ours again, so far as it is anybody's.
The annual long rental—essential to our economy for a hundred and fifty years—annually breaks its lease. Overnight,
traffic on Route 4 diminishes by thirty percent. A few elderly

Summer people remain, not forced back to Lincoln by school-opening or the end of vacation, but THEY move more cautiously now, nervous and polite or more nearly polite. THEY know THEY are outnumbered now. But with the growth of retirement condominium barn-palaces, we begin to witness in New Hampshire the newest phenomenon: year-round Summer people.

In Danbury the change is not so great as in some towns, because there are not so many Summer people. Yet the village celebrates the end of Summer, exodus and restoration, with the yearly Danbury Grange Harvest Festival and Parade, one Saturday soon after Labor Day. The harvest part is a show in the Legion Hall, melons and squash and tomatoes big and ripe, canning, pies—all displayed and judged. In the Grange Hall and Volunteer Fire Department there are crafts and sewing, watercolors, hot dogs and hamburgers, antiques, fudge, and penuche. In the afternoon horses compete at pulling weights and there is a baseball game; at five o'clock the Grange puts on its ham and bean supper.

The parade is the best part. We gather at the crossroads where 104 from Bristol and Plymouth hits Route 4 head on, between Danbury Center's two stores where Hippie Hill occupies the raised spot beside the railroad—no train for five years. The parade is decorated bicycles; the fife and drum corps from Bristol in Colonial costume; girls riding horseback; men driving antique cars; politicians standing upright in convertibles; floats from the Grange, the Fire Department, the South Danbury Christian Church, the Jiminy Cricket Kindergarten, and the Little League; Willard Huntoon leading his Holstein oxen; and seven or nine fire engines from Danbury and all the little towns hooting their sirens, the volunteers throwing fistfuls of candy out windows to children gathered at roadside.

After the Summer people have gone we enter a quiet time. Then at the end of September, throughout October and even into November, the leaf people come. They do not resemble

the Summer people. The leafers don't own, rent, or hold ten-
ancy here: They buy a ticket, as if for the Whirl-O-Ride at the
County Fair. Most of them elderly, they peer from bus windows with good will and mouths that make O's. Young leafers
from the flatlands drive their own cars and help support restaurant people, bed-and-breakfasters, inn-folks; for the tourist
business, leafers cut the wedge of a season between Summer
and Ski. They drive to the White Mountains in early September; later they mosey along little roads; they stop at the side of
Route 4 beside our barn to photograph yellow popple against
the gritty textures of unpainted vertical boards.

We like leaf people doubtless because we are also leaf people. In Andover down the road, the Lions club annually rents
a schoolbus and busdriver to take a load of Andover's senior
citizens up north. Because we are lucky enough to live here,
our ecstasy is annual, quotidian, and hysterical together, not
once-in-a-lifetime as it is for the riders of the great land yachts
with Texas license plates that wander for a week through
Green Mountains and White, parking where it says Scenic
View, where everybody whips out a Ph.D. camera (Push
Here, Dummy) and shoots the leaf's red dazzle for taking back
to Houston and San Antone. Sometimes these buses must have
trouble with their WCs, because Gail down at the Blackwater
Restaurant puts signs on her restrooms during leaf season, Out
of Order; it is uncanny what a busload of eighty senior citizens
can do for your septic system.

Fall is the time of the McIntosh.

Apples remain a big New Hampshire crop, after the other farming has pulled up and gone west. In our cellar the row of barrels remains where the squeezed apples took their long journey toward vinegar, important to the diet in decades when a single orange was a Christmas treat. It was always on the table—good with beets, canned or fresh, and with cabbage and with red-flannel hash, a north country soulfood that starts from the detritus of boiled dinner: Brown some salt pork in a skillet; grind up the leftover vegetables (cabbage, turnip, onion, potato, carrot); then grind up beets, which brings red flannel to the hash; and hash it together and serve it with a cruet of apple vinegar tapped from the cellar's barrel.

Our barrels have been dry, I suppose, for sixty years. The apple trees have gone that filled the barrels with cider and the bins with apples for the pies of Winter. We put in new trees now, midgets for easy picking: old varieties like Sheep's Nose which we chose for their names, some McIntosh for serious eating, Northern Spy and Strawberry . . . Down the road toward West Andover, the remains of the Blasington orchard still attract deer in the Autumn. Deer love apples—and hunters love abandoned orchards. Lately there are fewer deer, fewer hunters: An orchard a hundred years old loses flavor. For that matter, deer emigrate to the suburbs. Animals, like people, come and go, and deer follow the inhabitants who left, taking their cleared land with them. Two hundred years ago, when the farmers cut trees down for pasture and for grass, bear departed the cleared land for woods. Then the deer waxed. Now that farmers have left these narrow valleys, the deer wane and the woods return, bringing the bear back.

The farming that flourishes or endures in New Hampshire is special crop and part-time farming: People grow herbs and strawberries—or maybe apples. Great hillside orchards snow petals in Spring and dangle ripening fruit all Summer. At Bone's Orchard they grow thirty-seven varieties but ninety-eight percent of the apples they sell are Macs. Late Summer we drive past Bone's, watching the trees grow heavy with the dense globes of redness. We look for the day they start picking and later for the day they start pressing cider. Early Macs aren't much better than Delicious or Granny Smith; the lover of the true McIntosh lives for a short season. Brevity sweetens the flesh, and nothing is so intense to the mouth as a ripe McIntosh that detonates with the sweet-sweet yet acidy harsh texture of the accurate apple, Autumn's bounty. Or almost nothing. The textured flesh is a mouth's joy but the mouth or the mind's mouth craves the sweet torture of essence without texture, nervous pleasure-pain multiplied by abstraction: I mean *cider*.

The first taste of October's cider always recovers for me a single afternoon in the Autumn of 1944, a long walk with a new friend and a day I cherish. There are days in a long life that are carved without pain in the heart's chambers, or with pain as sweet as cider's. In September of 1944, I left home for the first time and lived among the barbarians of adolescence all day and night at a prep school in southern New Hampshire where I studied Latin in hopeless panic and wept tears of solitude and loathed the blond thicklipped sons of lawyers and brokers who glared at me with insolence, with frigidity, and without acknowledgment. Once I asked directions from someone who looked depressed—the only facial expression I wished to address—and when he proclaimed his ignorance we began our friendship to the death.

My new friend and I took a hike on a Sunday afternoon, walking for four hours maybe in a circle of dirt roads around the town, past grown-over farms and farms mothballed for war, on roads no one traveled because of gas rationing. It was dry and dusty but there was chill in the air, apple weather, and we walked smartly as we talked about everything important—the war, what we would do in the war, what we would do after the war and after college, our parents, our Goals in Life . . . Gradually and tentatively under the bright blue air we spoke with trust of what we most cared for. We walked under the bonny elms that had never heard of Dutch elm disease, under oaks still green, weathering toward gray, and under maples splendid with carmine. Worn out, heading back to school, we took a narrow road so quiet that it seemed as if we discovered it—teenage Magellans sailing the New Hampshire Fall, or maybe rediscovering it like a Mayan settlement grown over, for conquistadors to chance upon under jungle vines: architecture, temple, and aqueduct; for as we turned a curve we saw a great white farmhouse leading back from a wide lawn, and on the edge of the lawn at the dirt road's edge a table in the shade of an elm, empty glasses on it and a full tawny pitcher with a sign lettered on cardboard: CIDER 5¢ A GLASS.

It looked like the best idea the world ever came up with, cider in October on a dusty road, a miracle surely, and surely we were the first customers for thirty years or maybe a thousand . . . Then a screendoor banged on the porch above and a big old woman in a long housedress with a flowered apron over it worked her way over the grass, hobbling and smiling; she took our nickels and poured us cider; then she took a dime and poured us more cider; and then she took no more money but poured our glasses full until she emptied the pitcher.

We walked home as darkness started and red trees flared into the building dark. We walked with a light step in our friendship, tender and lively with the exquisite pain and excitement of cider wild in our mouths like apple fire. And if, thirty-five years later, my friend's wife found him prone on the staircase of their house, and if the lives lived have not entirely resembled the lives planned-for on a Sunday afternoon in 1944, at least the lives had that day in them, that house, that long friendship, and that cider.

In the old life of the farms, Fall was a lazy season. *Relatively*. Late in Fall the farmer cut down to eighty hours a week, maybe even to seventy-two.

First there was harvest. Come September my grandparents

dug potatoes for the cellar and buried late carrots in sand; come October they picked apples for cellar and ciderpress. The busiest time was bringing the fieldcorn in. My grandfather gathered it himself. The great grassy stalks, green as bamboo and thick, fell like soldiers in the teeth of the horsedrawn mowing machine; he always nailed the tallest, maybe twelve feet, on the barn door. Then the ensilage crew arrived early one morning. They brought with them the gasoline-powered cornchopper, a noisy rattling snarling belt-driven machine that gobbled whole stalks—white hard ears, green stalk, leaf and silk together. The machine blew the chopped mass into the silo, where my cousin Freeman tamped it down—Holstein granola for the milk of Winter and pale Spring.

When the fieldcorn was chopped and stowed, the machine disassembled and packed for its journey to the next farm, the hard part of the Fall was done with. There was fruit still to pick and cider to press. If no frost killed the plants there were tomatoes to can. After the first deep frost Kate and Wesley pulled up the remaining tomato plants to hang upside down in the shed where the green tomatoes blushed and turned edible. Now it was time to feed up the pig with corn for slaughter when it turned cold, to sell young roosters and wethers, to kill off old hens—one for dinner every Sunday—and settle pullets in the henhouse.

But none of these tasks was continuous, like haying all Summer or woodcutting in Winter. As soon as the grass stopped growing, cattle moved into the barn for Winter, standing all day in the tie-up eating golden hay, ensilage, and grain. Before heavy snow it was time for fencing, to walk the perimeters of the two pastures for cattle and sheep. Always there had been patching in the Summer when the sheep got out or maybe a cow or a heifer, or you could fence in July and August when the hay was too wet to bring in. But systematic fencing, mending wall as the poet says, occupied a few days between harvest and deer season; only suicidal farmers fenced during deer season. You hung a coil of wire over your shoulder, staples and hammer in overall pockets. Then you looked for places where a rock had tumbled loose or a tree, blown over in a thunder-storm, crashed across barbed wire. You set the stone back in place or chopped up the tree to clear the breach and strung more wire. And you looked around you in the October woods at the extended private exhibition, low pale Autumn sunlight striking through the diminishing leafy air to catch on reds and yellows of the great woods. After hauling rocks it was good to catch your breath; it was good to look, and look, and look.

And everyone looked and still *looks*. Even people who have lived their whole lives here never become bored with this look-ing—the old farmers I remember; my cousins now. When I was young I thought maybe the old didn't see, didn't relish the beauty they lived in. Then I learned: For more than a hundred years, anybody willing to leave this countryside has been re-warded for leaving it by more money, leisure, and creature comforts. A few may have stayed from fecklessness or lack of gumption; more have stayed from family feeling or homesick-ness; but most stay from love. I live among a population, ex-traordinary in our culture, that lives where it lives because it loves its place. We are self-selected place-lovers. There's no reason to live here except for love.

At Halloween the mounded pumpkins of the roadside, carved, grin with candles from all the doorsteps, and the stuffed guys of the dooryards and all the ghosts of Summer gather at Oc-

tober's end. According to the calendar, Winter begins just before Christmas Eve, at the solstice of the twenty-second, but the
soul's calendar, like the body's, knows that Autumn dwindles
by entropy into Winter as Halloween turns the corner to November. In November we rake leaves for insulation against the
sides of the house, as the grandfathers and great-grandfathers
did forever in their northern houses, heaping the Summer's
warmth against the foundation stones and low clapboards.

Winter's onset is the theme of Autumn after the glory's
gone. Ice forms in the watering trough; we scrape ice from
the windshield early in the morning. In the pale grays and
browns of late October and November we tuck the house up,
tamping her skirts down and bundling her tight against
the winds of thirty below. We split and stack cordwood in the
woodshed, splinter-time, packing the Autumn wood as we
used to pack hay in the Summer's rick. Now the house's Fall
puts on weight and solidity, like the bear fattening himself
for a long Winter's sleep, and the house is protected by the collapsed Summer's dead leaves, forearmed with firewood that
is the stored heat of many Summers turned into fiber by sun
and rain through the agency of leaves. Trees warm the wooden
house.

Thanksgiving's turkey is the Fall's last Fall: "Over the river
and through the wood / To grandfather's house we go . . ."
The horse knows the way, and so does the Nissan pick-up.
Though the turkey be frozen and the stuffing be Pepperidge
Farm, the Pilgrims' late celebration of corn and apple and
cranberry, of mince and turnip and cider, turns the last key
in the door of Autumn. At noon the potato mashes and the
gravy thickens. In early dark we lie about, with football break-
ing its bones all over the living room, and we make Thanksgiving for one more cycle of the year gone through, ended with
the great ghostdance of Autumn, bright and pale wedded from
September's leaf to November's early dark.

And although we may regret the darkening day, the beauty
of late Autumn is real and serious. With the leaves down, gran-

ite emerges from the hills, and everywhere we see again the hills' true shape and the stonewalls that the ancestors built — to enclose their animals and to clear their fields of rocks — making gray rectangles on the gray hillsides.

Late October or early November — after weeks of frost and the fields brown and the harvest long taken and the garden ripped up and dumped and the trees mostly bare and the house tucked up for Winter — comes the moment of miraculous restoration, Summer's curtain call or triumphal final tour: The wind relents, the sun rises, golden warmth risen from frozen acres, and Indian Summer visits like a millionaire; the expensive stranger walks over Kearsarge and Ragged and spends gold sunshine on the unreceptive fields. Down jackets hang again from a brief hook; the Summer's T-shirt reappears. Flies wake in the windows of the second storey; a wasp rubs her lazy legs together. If the frost has not finished them, late asters and chrysanthemums hover in summery air along with other late survivors: maybe the spindly autumnal goldenrod. Soon, sure enough, frost will blacken Fall's flowers and snow tamp them down with its orgy of sensuous deprivation, but now for five days or seven they float a warm raft of mid-Summer on the lake of Fall's desolation.

SEASONS AT EAGLE POND

was typeset by Heritage Printers in Linotype Waverley, a face based on the designs of Justus Erich Walbaum, a nineteenth-century German typefounder. The woodcut illustrations by Thomas W. Nason were reproduced from prints in the collection of the Boston Public Library. The book was designed by Anne Chalmers and was printed and bound by The Book Press, Brattleboro, Vermont.